IMAGES OF ENGLAND

INNS AND TAVERNS OF NORTH SHIELDS

IMAGES OF ENGLAND

INNS AND TAVERNS OF NORTH SHIELDS

CHARLIE STEEL

TEMPUS

Frontispiece: The Spread Eagle is in the foreground, with the Bamburgh Castle Inn beyond (Preston Township, *c.* 1906).

Page six: Looking north along a narrow, cobbled Clive Street, *c.* 1905.

First published 2007

Tempus Publishing
Cirencester Road, Chalford
Stroud, Gloucestershire, GL6 8PE
www.tempus-publishing.com

Tempus Publishing is an imprint of NPI Media Group

British Library Cataloguing in Publication Data.
A catalogue record for this book is available from the British Library.

ISBN 978 07524 4365 2

Typesetting and origination by NPI Media Group.
Printed in Great Britain.

Contents

Acknowlegements

It is only with the assistance and encouragement of others that the compilation of this book has been possible, so I am particularly grateful to the under mentioned organisations and people who have contributed in various ways:

Tyne & Wear Archives, Blenheim Street, Newcastle-upon-Tyne
Alan Hildrew, North Shields Local Studies Library
Betty Steel, Monkseaton
Colin Wilkinson, Preston Village, North Shields
Ron Wright, Cullercoats
Susan Little, Murton Village
Margaret Appleby, the Spread Eagle, Preston Village
Fred Turnbull, the Ship Inn, Monkseaton
Diane Montague, the Sportsman Inn, Preston Village
Hugh Price, Tynemouth Lodge Hotel, North Shields
Lillian and Arthur Reeve, The Porthole, North Shields
Andrew Hickson, Rockcliffe Arms, Whitley Bay
Anthony Smithson, Keel Row Bookshop, North Shields

SOURCES OF REFERENCE
Pigots Directories 1822–1834
Parson & Whites Directories 1827–1828
Wards Directories 1850–1940
Whellans Directory 1855
Bulmers Directory 1887
Kellys Directories 1894–1938
Blairs County of Northumberland Directories 1968
Northumberland Census Records
Ordnance Survey maps
Licensing Registers
A History of the Pubs & Inns of North Tyneside, by Kevin Bradley
English Inns, by Thomas Burke
The Northumbrian Pub, by Lynn F. Pearson
North Shields and Tynemouth, by Richard Simpson
Licensed Premises – Law and Practice, by Philip Kolvin

Introduction

Preparation of this book has involved many hours of research, trawling through old directories and licensing records to compile what I consider to be a comprehensive list or gazetteer of all the inns, taverns, alehouses, hotels and beer sellers recorded in North Shields and its surrounding environs from 1822 to the present day. Many of the known independent brewers, beer sellers and merchants have also been included as a separate section, but are not included within the main body of the book.

Of course, old records cannot be relied on to be entirely accurate and I therefore apologise to the reader for any errors or omissions which may become apparent – there are bound to be a few, particularly in relation to some of the dates which should be referred to only as a basic guide. The oldest directory I have been able to use during my research is dated 1822, and therefore this has been used as a general starting point for some of the older premises listed in this book: however, many of them will have been built or indeed established long before that date.

In using this book, it will also be noted that many addresses shown for the same premises will differ, and this is attributable to various factors. Over the years, Tynemouth Council introduced a renumbering system of streets in the borough, which effectively meant that many premises were subject to an enforced change of postal address. For example, the Alnwick Castle pub is shown as 26 and 28 Saville Street, as well as 22 and 112 Church Way, North Shields.

This is an example where the street number of the premises is that under which it was recorded during different years, and quite often buildings which stood on a corner site would sometimes be listed in directories as appearing on either one or both of those streets, which in turn may also have been subject to renumbering, hence the apparent discrepancies. Sometimes, road or street names would change, or they may have been better known by a local name. For example: Albion Street became Albion Road, and Lower Pearson Street became Charlotte Street.

Some streets were sub-named, such as Cobourg Terrace, which forms part of Tynemouth Road. Sometimes, there would be anomalies where a continuous road began or ended, such as in the Low Town where Clive Street continued into Liddell Street, which in turn merged with Bell Street, only to become Union Street or Union Quay within a short distance.

Many inns and taverns themselves have undergone several name changes over a period of time, and combined with apparent address changes, this has made it difficult to establish and confirm the identity of many of the older individual pubs with any degree of certainty. Also, some of the older directories used for compilation were not always 100 per cent accurate in their content, and therefore allowances need to be taken into consideration for possible errors.

As a relatively small town in the 1800s, North Shields has probably had the highest number of inns, taverns, alehouses and beer sellers to be found anywhere in the country. The Low Town in particular had an extremely high concentration of pubs, with some inns actually adjoining the next one, and others just being a matter of feet away from the next.

Between 1822 and the present day, approximately 440 inns, taverns and alehouses have been recorded in North Shields, with over 110 additional premises in the surrounding areas, covering a time span of almost 200 years. These numbers do not include the small independent ale, porter, wine and spirit merchants and brewers, which themselves number in excess of 225. The largest volume of public houses was approximately 180 in North Shields High Town, 158 in the Low Town, and 83 in the west end and Bull Ring area of the town. The Chirton and Percy Main areas comprised around seventeen public houses, and Preston Township had fourteen known inns and taverns.

Over the years, Tynemouth was well catered for, with around thirty-four establishments, and moving north up the coastline to Cullercoats there are eleven recorded here, including the modern premises on Marden Estate. Next was Whitley Bay (Whitley Township), which had around twenty-four inns, taverns and hotels, but that excludes any of the modern theme bars in the South Parade area which tend to change their names on a regular basis, and strictly speaking, cannot be considered as true pubs anyway.

Monkseaton Village has had eight inns and taverns over the years, and Earsdon Village has had six. The Backworth and Shiremoor areas, including New York and Murton Village, had twelve licensed premises. (It should however be remembered that not all of these premises existed at any one time).

If new information comes to light, or inaccuracies are identified, I would be pleased to hear about them so that they might be corrected and incorporated in any future reprint.

Charlie Steel
May 2007

A History of North Shields

In 1225, the Prior of Tynemouth built twenty-seven huts or 'Shielings' in which to house his workers at the Pow Burn, situated to the east of the present Fish Quay. This small settlement rapidly grew to a thriving township of over 100 dwellings, and by the end of the thirteenth century included a quay landing, wharves, a brewery, mills and bakehouses, and so the development of North Shields began. The origin of the name North Shields is somewhat uncertain, but it is probable that it was derived from these 'Shielings', which were often referred to as 'Sheels' on the north side of the river.

It has often been said that the best way to learn history is to study castles and churches; however it cannot be denied that the best way to learn about the history of North Shields is to study the pubs! In 1853, it was estimated that there were 217 public houses, taverns and alehouses in the Borough of Tynemouth, which included North Shields, Tynemouth and Cullercoats.

North Shields itself consists of two parts: the High Town and the Low Town. The High Town was basically the town centre and the area above the river that was built on the 'High Ground'. The Low Town comprised all the buildings, streets, quays and stairs below the High Town, and ran down the steep banks to the riverside, from near the site of the present Tanners Bank to the New Quay, with many of the quays here actually deriving their names from people or local inns.

The narrow winding streets running parallel with the river, and running from east to west, made up Union Road, Union Quay, Western Quay, Bell Street, Liddell Street, Clive Street and Duke Street, which in some places were so tight that it was only possible for one horse and cart to pass through at a time.

Houses, shops and inns were crowded against each other along the streets, and access to the river was via narrow alleyways and quays. Dozens of stairs lined the steep banks to connect the Low Town with the High Town, and provided access to the hundreds of crowded tenement buildings which were constructed along the length of the bank sides. These buildings were nothing more than slums, infested with rats and vermin, and even as far back as the mid-1800s they were recorded as being nothing more than the refuge of scum and the lowest dregs of society.

In the 1700s and 1800s, the Low Town was rife with petty thieves and prostitutes and could be a dangerous and formidable place. The area was generally out of bounds for any self-respecting citizen, especially during the hours of darkness as muggings were widespread, crime was common, and press gangs were known to scour the waterfront to find suitable men for conscription and impressment.

There was a high concentration of public houses in the Low Town of North Shields, where at one time, there were sixteen pubs on Clive Street alone, stretching alphabetically from the Bay Horse to the Waterloo. Many of the taverns and alehouses in this area were dirty, seedy drinking dens of vice and intemperance, dimly lit with tallow candles, where drunkenness was commonplace and many unlawful and immoral schemes were plotted. Most of these dens of iniquity have long since disappeared, and by 2007, the only old establishments left in the Low Town were the New Dolphin, the Low Lights, the Prince of Wales and the Golden Fleece (now renamed The Porthole).

Despite its reputation, North Shields was recognised as a thriving and bustling fishing port, but during the twentieth century, quayside activities declined, and as a result, many of the old buildings and concentrated masses of tenement houses and slums that once filled the bank sides were demolished, leaving only a few plaques, which serve as a reminder to indicate the sites of many of the old quays and stairs.

Although the streets of the Low Town still exist to this day, it can be difficult to imagine how the area looked during the 1800s – those dark days of North Shields Low Town are now long gone, most of the area is virtually unrecognisable today, whilst a programme of redevelopment progresses. Much of the old Low Town is now overlooked by modern houses, flats and apartments, and has become a popular venue with families who visit the restaurants, shops and attractions now lining the riverside and Fish Quay areas. Since these early beginnings, North Shields has grown into the town it is today, leaving a wealth of history behind it.

ORIGINS OF BEER

It is difficult to determine where ale was first brewed. Certainly it was known in the Tigris and Euphrates valleys before 4000 BC and it was known to the Babylonians in 2300 BC, for one of their laws stated that a priestess going into an alehouse to drink could be burned alive as a punishment. It is also said to have been introduced into Egypt by the god Osiris or his divine spouse Isis in 2017 BC. Beer was an important part of the Egyptian diet.

Neither is it known whether the inhabitants of Britain brewed ale before the Roman invasion – but they were certainly doing so when the Romans left. The establishment of the Roman road network created the first inns, in which the weary traveller could obtain refreshment, and so the beginnings of the modern pub had been established. They became so commonplace that in AD 965 King Edgar decreed that there should be no more than one alehouse per village.

During the Roman occupation glass beakers and bowls were used for drinking, but later, the art of glass making was lost, so earthenware pots and drinking horns were used. Mazers or wooden drinking cups were also in use, as were 'tumblers' – leather cups that had a rounded bottom and so tumbled over when they were put down. There were also peg-tankards, which held about two quarts. Pegs inside the tankard divided the contents into eight parts so that each drinker, as the tankard was passed from hand to hand, had only his fair share: hence the expression, 'to have a peg'. There were also, in the Middle Ages, leather blackjacks. These were leather containers, of one-pint size, the insides of which had been treated with pitch. Mention must also be made of the bombard, a vessel made for the really mighty drinker, which could hold anything up to fifteen quarts! Of course, wealthy people drank from magnificently ornamented and jewelled cups and goblets of silver and gold.

In the year 1266 it was decided to regulate the price of ale by that of barley, and it is recorded that when barley was 2s for 512 pounds in weight, ale was a farthing a quart. This was at a time when a labourer earned about 9d a day. It is interesting to note that in those days ale was the general drink, being drunk at all times by young and old alike. Servants, for instance, both male and female, usually had a piece of bread and a quart of ale for breakfast. In fact it is recorded, just after the Norman invasion, that the Canons of St Paul's had a personal ration of 30 gallons of ale each week.

This great consumption of ale may seem rather odd today, but it should be remembered that in those days there was nothing else to drink. Tea, coffee and cocoa were unknown and very little ordinary water was fit to drink unless one was fortunate enough to live near a natural spring or a small country stream. In addition, it should be remembered that food was neither so plentiful nor varied as it is today, and as ale is a great source of nourishment as well as energy it was naturally a staple part of the diet.

It was not until the reign of Charles I that ale was taxed, and his son Charles II further increased the tax in 1660 until it was 1s 3d a barrel on small beer. It is not known when beer was first brewed – you will have noticed that up until now the word 'ale' has been exclusively used. The difference between the two is that ale was brewed only from malt, whereas beer was brewed from malt and hops. Be that as it may, the word 'beer' was in common use by the year 1524 so it must have been some considerable time before that.

New taxes were continually added to this indispensable beverage until they reached 4.5d a gallon before being repealed in 1830. The first bottled beer was produced in the seventeenth century and it was an exceptionally strong beer, which was called stout. Porter was also first brewed about this time and was a cross between stout and beer. It is interesting to note that until the middle of the fifteenth century the majority of brewing was done in the home.

In *The English Housewife*, published early in the seventeenth century, the following passage occurs: 'It is most requisite and fit that the Housewife be experienced and well practiced in the well making of malt, for as from it is made the drink by which the household is nourished and sustained'. As a result of this home brewing very little was done on a commercial scale and in 1585 there were only twenty-six brewers in London and its surroundings. However, when tea arrived in England from the Far East early in the seventeenth century and rapidly became a favourite drink among all classes, home brewing started to wane, so that by 1685 there were 200 brewers in London and nearly 700 in the rest of the country.

It is interesting to note that Trumans and Whitbread's were among the well-known early London brewers, as were Bass and Worthington among the Burton brewers. As time passed the commercial brewers grew larger and many of them amalgamated and, with the advance of science, the art of brewing became exact instead of being, as it had for hundreds of years, merely a matter of rule of thumb.

For over a thousand years ale or beer was the staple drink of all the inhabitants of the British Isles but gradually this deep-rooted habit gave way before the onslaught of cheaper tea, coffee and cocoa, while the growth of many temperance societies banished it from numerous homes. There are, naturally, many arguments for and against beer but most of those against it seem to stem from ignorance or prejudice and possibly the excesses of the few. The plain and truthful fact is that beer is, as our forefathers well knew, a health-giving and invigorating beverage and one that even today, with its high taxation and comparatively low gravity, is still cheap.

For instance, as a drink taken at any time, it has double the calorie value of the same quantity of tea or coffee. It also greatly enhances the value of any meal. Compare the average meal of today consisting of soup, beef, potatoes, cabbage, gravy and coffee with the old fashioned lunch of a pint of beer, three or four slices of buttered bread with cheese and a bit of lettuce, and two very startling facts emerge. The first is that it is an incontrovertible medical fact that the latter is a perfectly balanced meal in every way, which is more than can be said for the stodgy cooked meal. To put it in its simplest possible form, a pint of beer has the same energy-giving value as four eggs or more than half a pound of meat!

Burton-on-Trent has been famous for ale and beer for many centuries. This is because, among other things, the water in this district has a high gypsum content, which renders it ideal for brewing. Burton ale was known in the time of Richard *Coeur de Lion* and the ale brewed in Burton Abbey was famed for its excellence. Indeed, it was the ale from this abbey that was supplied to Mary, Queen of Scots, when she was imprisoned in Tutbury Castle in 1580. It was not until the reign of George III, however, that the first commercial brewery was established at Burton by one Benjamin Printon. A few years later the owner of a cartage business decided that he would sooner make beer than cart it and so, in 1777, he took over the brewery of Benjamin Printon. The carter's name was William Bass.

It is very interesting to note that the present-day 'Bottle of Bass' largely owes its origin to an accident. In 1797, twenty years after the inception of the firm, the annual trade amounted to 2,000 barrels, a good proportion of which was exported to Russia, Finland and Poland, for in those days it was cheaper to send the beer by sea to Russia than by road to London! This export trade, however, was practically eliminated in 1822 by a prohibitive tariff and so, looking round for other suitable markets, Mr Bass decided to produce a pale ale suitable for the Far East. Unfortunately – or should it be fortunately? – a shipment on its way to India was wrecked in the Irish Channel and some of the salvaged casks of beer were sold in Liverpool. The quality of this special beer was so appreciated that the fame of 'East India Pale Ale' spread rapidly, with the result that it was soon put on the home market.

'Bass' is made using the finest quality barley soaked in cold water in steeping tanks for about three days. The water is then drained off and the barley is spread out on the malt-house floor to allow germination to begin. When germination has progressed to the required degree, the barley is moved to a kiln. This is a large room with a floor of finely perforated tiles through which heat can be brought to bear, so arresting germination and at the same time drying the barley, which at this stage becomes known as malt. The malt is then sent to the brewery and fed into crushing mills.

The grist, as it is now called, is then mixed with hot water and run into mash tuns. Here it is allowed to infuse in exactly the same way that tea is made. Unlike tea, however, certain natural changes take place at this stage, such as the starches being turned into malt sugars. When the infusion is completed the resultant clear liquid, known as wort, is run off. This process can be repeated using the same grist, in exactly the same way that a second pot of tea can be made from the first lot of tea leaves with exactly the same result – the second infusion is weaker than the first. It is, in fact, this second brew that was, in medieval times, known as 'small beer'.

After the wort has been run off, the mash tun is sprayed with water, or 'sparged', until all the extract is taken from the malt. And here it might be said the basic difference in brewing between the various grades and qualities of beer is purely a question of gravity: the stronger the beer, the more malt and less water is used, and, conversely, for weaker beers, less malt and more water. Hops have no effect on gravity and are added in the proportions appropriate to the different brews to attain the quality desired.

From the mash tun the wort is run off into a large vessel known as an underback from which it is run into coppers where it is mixed with hops and boiled. The hops, until wanted, are stored in huge cold stores in which the temperature is kept at 2 degrees of frost. On leaving the coppers, the wort passes through a large vessel called a hop-back which is, in effect, a giant strainer which strains off the spent hops leaving the liquid clear again. The wort then runs into a cooler and through various refrigerators whereby it is cooled as rapidly as possible. Some aeration also takes place at this stage. From the refrigerators the wort flows into the fermentation vessels. Here, yeast is added and fermentation takes place, the yeast breaking down the malt sugars in the wort and converting them into alcohol. Although many bottled beers are aerated with carbonic acid gas to give a sparkling drink with a good head, the effervescence found in a bottle of Bass is the result of a completely natural process.

Such is the story of ale and beer, a story over 6,000 years old, a story which is still being told and sung the world over. Cheers!!!

THE ENGLISH PUB

When the first English road was built, the first English inn was born. The date of that event, no man knows, but from that day to this, the inn, tavern, alehouse and pub have been an essential part of English life as well as a delightful feature of the English scene. In England, a visitor needing directions is usually guided to his destination not by churches or street names, but by pub names.

With one in almost every village, the term 'pub' or 'public house' is a general term used to describe any inn, tavern or alehouse, of which there are now approximately 60,000 in the United Kingdom. In many places, a pub can be the focal point of the community, playing a similar role to the local church in this respect.

The old coaching inns also played an important role in days gone by, and can usually be identified by a large arched entrance leading to a courtyard, where stabling for horses and accommodation facilities were provided to the traveller. In one way or another, and throughout history, the English pub has been placed at the heart of our social culture, as they tend to be a canvas against which the drama of our daily lives is played out. Relationships are made and broken, sorrows drowned, and successes toasted. Whatever the occasion or reason, it is because we are a nation that likes to drink.

At the time of the Norman Conquest, William of Malmesbury wrote: 'Drinking in particular is a universal practice, in which occupation entire nights as well as days are passed away. The English were accustomed to eat till they became surfeited, and drank until they were sick.' The English defeat at the hands of the Norman invader was put down to drink, the natives fighting more with rashness and precipitate fury than with military skill. The writer and presenter Jeremy Paxman once stated that 'the English, far from being ashamed of their behaviour, see fighting and drunkenness as part of their birthright. It is the way they proclaim their identity'.

The historic role of the English drinking establishment is, however, seen as a place of entertainment, accommodation and for the transaction of commerce. In 1606, King James I passed two pieces of legislation, for the licensing of alehouses and the suppression of drunkenness. The title of the latter proclaimed its noble purpose: 'An Act for Repressing the Odious and Loathsome Sin of Drunkenness'. The legislation conspicuously failed, because further legislation was introduced in 1609: 'An Act for the Reformation of Alehouse Keepers'.

The monarch continued his programme of reform, which led to the first recorded example of licensing hours: the Newmarket Proclamation of James I in 1618. This required all inns and alehouses to close at 9 p.m. and also during divine service on Sundays. During the protectorate of Oliver Cromwell (1653-1658), King James imposed closure throughout Sundays, but the restrictions seem to have lapsed thereafter. While justices took it upon themselves to impose closing times, no national hours or days of trade were set again until 1839. By the end of the seventeenth century, there was very little control over the supply of liquor, with licences freely granted by the justices, and rarely withdrawn, causing an expansion in the number of licensed premises, and the consumption of beer to increase by 1722 to thirty-six gallons a year for every man, woman and child.

At the end of the eighteenth century, licensing curtailments were imposed by Pitts' government in the 'Royal Proclamation against Vice' of 1757, passed against growing concerns that many licensed premises were becoming dens of iniquity, as well as places for the unemployed to plan their crimes. The proclamation declared the royal intention to punish 'all manner of vice, profaneness and immorality'. It forbade gambling on Sundays and urged strict enforcement of laws against 'excessive drinking, blasphemy, profane swearing or cursing, lewdness, profanation of the Lords Day, or other dissolute, immoral or disorderly practices.'

In the early nineteenth century, there was a vast increase in alcohol consumption, particularly gin, and in 1830, the Duke of Wellington's Beer Act abolished duty on beer and ales in the hope of weaning some of the working classes off spirits, and an amazing 24,000 new beer-shop licences were granted during the first year of the act, rising to 46,000 by 1836, and the number of public houses increased by 15 per cent within ten years of this legislation.

The growth of public houses in England continued, and probably reached its peak during the latter half of the 1800s: however, the past 100 years have seen a decline in numbers, although their popularity has never weakened. The style of the English pub has changed dramatically over the years. At one time, a pub was simply a place to do little else but drink ale and engage in social merriment; however the traditional pub is at a serious risk of being lost as the commercial sector have seized on the opportunity to make vast profits by converting pubs into restaurants where a huge emphasis is put on high volume food sales rather than quality ales.

Many other establishments have been converted to uncomfortable and unappealing theme bars with 'happy hours' and standing room only, or mini leisure centres where entire families can allegedly be 'entertained' with indoor and outdoor playgrounds, music, dancing, fruit machines, gaming machines, quizzes, and large-screen televisions, whilst many of the old-established and traditional bar games such as skittles, darts, dominoes, cribbage and even 'shove-ha'penny' have fallen into decline.

Fizzy mass-produced pasteurised beers, lagers and 'alcopops' are now commonplace, with many noted names being consumed only because it is fashionable to drink certain brands from a bottle. This may have contributed to a change in the drinking culture, particularly amongst younger people, which has led to concerns by the government over excessive alcohol consumption and so-called 'binge-drinking'. Fortunately, there are still a good number of traditional pubs left where the demand for real ales is high, and for much of this, we need to be thankful to CAMRA (the Campaign for Real Ale), who have been instrumental in promoting and retaining this tradition over the past few years.

The owner, tenant or manager (licensee) of a public house is known as the publican or landlord. In the UK a 'tied house' is a public house that is required to buy at least some of its beer from a particular brewery, unlike 'free houses', which are able to choose the beers they stock freely.

The pub itself may be owned by the brewery in question, with the publican renting the pub from the brewery: this is termed a tenancy. Alternatively, the brewery may appoint a salaried manager to run the pub it owns: this form of tie can sometimes be termed a managed house. Finally, a publican may finance the purchase of a pub with soft loans from a brewer, and be required to buy his beer from them in return.

The traditional advantage of tied houses for breweries was the steady demand they gave them – a tied house would not change its beers suddenly, so the brewer had a consistent market for their beer. However, this sometimes could victimise consumers, as when a regional brewer tied nearly every pub in an area, so it became very hard to drink anything but their beer. This was a form of monopoly opposed by CAMRA, especially when the brewer forced poor beer onto the market, due to the lack of competition from better breweries.

Some or all drinks are then supplied by the brewery including spirits and soft drinks, quite often at an uncompetitive price relative to those paid by free houses. Since 1989 tied pubs in the UK have been legally permitted to stock at least one guest beer from another brewery to give greater choice to drinkers.

At one time, beer and ale was supplied from various-sized vessels of a set capacity, the names of which tend to be largely unheard of these days. They were colourfully referred to as follows:

Tun:	A large vessel containing 252 gallons.
Butt:	A smaller vessel containing 108 gallons.
Hogshead:	(Equivalent to half a butt), containing 54 gallons.
Barrel:	(A size of cask or keg), containing 36 imperial gallons.
Kilderkin:	(A half-barrel), containing 18 gallons.
Firkin:	(A quarter barrel), containing 9 gallons.
Polypin:	(Half a Firkin or 36 pints).
Quart:	2 pints or a quarter gallon.

ORIGINS OF PUB NAMES

Throughout Britain, many of the older public houses and hostelries are suffixed with 'tavern', 'inn', 'hotel', 'vaults', 'house', 'arms' or 'head'. In the past, a sharp distinction was drawn between the tavern and the inn, as they were controlled by laws peculiar to each other, and held a different form of licence. The tavern was restricted to providing casual refreshment, both food and drink, and was usually kept by a vintner. The inn was restricted to the receipt and entertainment of travellers and wayfarers by day and by night, along with the provision of accommodation. Neither was allowed to overlap the other. The tavern was forbidden to harbour guests; the inn was forbidden to allow itself to be used for 'tippling' or as a place of idle resort. The tavern had to close at a certain hour, whereas the inn had to be open at all hours.

Today, there is no distinction between the two for the purpose of licensing, as it is widely accepted that their functions are much the same. Nowadays most inns as part of their ordinary business provide the service given by the taverns of the past, and many taverns or public houses give the service that was once restricted to the inn.

The larger inns usually became 'hotels', the strict definition of which is an establishment providing accommodation and meals for travellers. Other suffixes applied to public house names, along with their respective definitions are:

Vaults: A room or space with arched walls and ceilings, especially underground, such as a cellar, basement or store-room.

House: A building having a particular function, or providing a particular service to the public.

Arms: Heraldic bearings or insignia, as of a state, official, place, family or organisation.

Head: The upper end or extremity of something: Foremost in importance: Placed at the top or front.

Beyond these definitions, the titles or names of many public houses usually have a story behind them, the origin of which came about in 1393, when King Richard II of England compelled landlords to erect signs outside their premises. The legislation stated: 'Whosoever shall brew ale in the town with intention of selling it must hang out a sign; otherwise he shall forfeit his ale'. The reason for this was to make them easily visible to passing inspectors of the quality of the ale they provided (during this period, drinking water was not always good to drink and ale was the usual replacement).

Another important factor was that during the Middle Ages a large percentage of the population would have been illiterate and so pictures were more useful than words as a means of identifying a public house. For this reason there was often no reason to write the establishment's name on the sign and inns opened without a formal written name – the name being derived later from the illustration on the public house's sign. In this sense, a pub sign can be thought of as an early example of visual branding. Instead of a painted sign, some publicans would identify their establishment by hanging or standing a distinctive object outside the pub, such as a boot, a copper kettle or a crooked billet (a branch from a tree).

In the modern era most British pubs still have highly decorated signs hanging over their doors, and these retain their original function of enabling the rapid identification of the public house – a memorable and prominently located pub sign is still an important means of picking up passing trade. Today's pub signs almost always bear the name of the pub, both in words and in pictorial representation.

Although the word 'the' appears on much public house signage, it is not considered to be an important part of the name. Likewise, the word 'ye' should also be ignored as it is only another version of 'the', and alternative spellings such as 'olde' are simply a derivation of a modern spelling.

Interesting origins are not confined to old or traditional names, and some modern names are often nothing more than a marketing ploy frequently using amusing themes considered to be memorable, such as 'Slug and Lettuce'. Elements of pub names, and their origins, can be broken up into a relatively small number of categories, so to provide a better understanding of this, some local examples are indicated and explained under the following appropriate headings:

Alcohol Related Pub Names
Barley Mow (Clive Street, North Shields): barley is laid in a malting, heated and watered until the grain germinates. The grain is then cooked which kills the germination process and the result is called

malt. Malt is the ingredient in beer which gives it its sweet taste and colour. The mow is a stack.

Three Tuns (Wooden Bridge, North Shields): a tun is a large cask for liquids, especially wine, or a mash tun is an insulated vessel with a false bottom used in brewing. The three tuns are based on the arms of both the Worshipful Company of Vinters and the Worshipful Company of Brewers (City of London Guilds).

Heraldry

Heraldry was a fundamental element in naming pubs, and examples of items appearing on a coat of arms, would be:

Red Lion (Earsdon Village and Church Way, North Shields): originally an armorial symbol of John of Gaunt, this became the most common inn name in England when James I decreed that the Stuart Red Lion be displayed throughout the kingdom. Although it was widely recognised as a Scottish emblem, many innkeepers acknowledged the royal proposal and adopted the name.

White Hart (Bedford Street, North Shields): the white hart was the emblem of King Richard II of England. It became extremely popular as an inn sign in his reign, and was adopted by many later inns and taverns.

Historic Events

Saracen's Head (Liddell Street, North Shields): tales of the Crusades handed down over generations led to variations on the Christian endeavours to convert the Muslim Middle East; the Saracen was a brave warrior from this region.

Turk's Head (Duke Street and Linskill Street, North Shields and Front Street, Tynemouth): also a reference to the warriors of that region, again as a result of the Crusades.

Rose and Crown (Liddell Street and Tyne Street, North Shields): after the Battle of Bosworth Field in which King Richard III was killed, the victor Henry Tudor proclaimed himself King Henry VII. Henry had no real claim to the throne of England, so had to legitimise his position. This he did by marrying someone who did have a claim: Princess Elizabeth of York. She was so beautiful she was known as the Rose of York. Hence the commemorating pub name: the Rose is Princess Elizabeth; the Crown Henry VII.

Royal Oak (Bell Street and Mount Pleasant, North Shields): after the Battle of Worcester in 1651 during the English Civil War, the defeated Prince Charles escaped the scene with the Roundheads on his tail. He managed to reach Shifnal in Shropshire, where he found an oak tree (now known as the Boscobel Oak). He climbed the tree and hid in it for a day while the obviously short-sighted Parliamentarians strolled around under the tree looking for him. After the hunters gave up, Prince Charles came down and escaped to France. He became King Charles II on the Restoration of the Monarchy. To celebrate this good fortune, 29 May (Charles' birthday) was declared Royal Oak Day and the pub's name commemorates this. The Royal Naval ship gets its name from the same source.

Hunting and Blood Sports

The Cock (Clive Street, North Shields).

Foxhunters (Preston North Road, Preston).

The Greyhound (Church Street, Bell Street, Toll Street and Bird Street, North Shields).

Falcon Arms (Dotwick Street).

Landowners
Many names with 'Arms' as a suffix, refer to the local landowner. This usually makes such names unique.

Location
An 'Arms' name can also be derived from where the premises are situated, for example: the **'Monkseaton Arms'** (Monkseaton) or the **'Borough Arms'** (Borough Road). Likewise, the site of a pub can have a bearing on the name, such as the **Corner House** (Bull Ring, North Shields), standing on a corner or road junction.

Old Hundred (Albion Road, North Shields): at one time, the address was 100 Church Way.

High Point Hotel (The Promenade, Whitley Bay): named because of its prominent position high on the seafront.

Myths and Legends
Phoenix (Bedford Street, Clive Street and Earsdon Village): a mythical bird that dies in flames and is reborn from the ashes.

Green Man (Liddell Street, North Shields): the spirit of the woods. The original images are in churches as a face peering through leaves and petals; this character is the Will o' the Wisp. Some pub signs will also show the Green Man as he appears in English traditional sword dances (in green tats). The Green Man may also be linked to the legend of Robin Hood.

Robin Hood (Front Street, Chirton and Murton Village): probably the most famous of English heroes. A man who fought the repressive ruling regime of the day or to put it simply – he stole from the rich to give to the poor. According to popular legends, Robin Hood was based (with his band of Merry Men) in Sherwood Forest which is sited north of Nottingham.

Occupations
Some 'Arms' signs refer to working occupations. These may show a trade or profession and some examples are the **'Artillery Arms'** (Albion Road), or the **'Cordwainers Arms'** (Bell Street).

Personal Names or Titles
Marquis of Granby (Church Street, North Shields): John Manners, Marquis of Granby, was a general in the eighteenth century. He showed a great concern for the welfare of his men upon their retirement and provided funds for many to establish taverns, which were subsequently named after him.

Prince of Wales (Liddell Street and Union Street, North Shields): royalty, i.e. the Prince of Wales.

Lord Nelson (Camden Street, North Shields): Horatio Nelson, the victorious admiral, was born at Burnham Thorpe, Norfolk. It is traditional to name pubs after Britain's war heroes and so Nelson is an obvious subject.

Shakespeare (Clive Street, Howard Street and Lishman's Quay, North Shields): William Shakespeare was an English poet and playwright who had a number of inns named after him throughout the country.

Places

Tyne Inn (Camden Street and Tennyson Terrace, North Shields): named after the river Tyne connection.

Northumberland Hotel (New Quay, North Shields and Percy Square, Tynemouth): named after the County of Northumberland.

Raby Castle (Tyne Street, North Shields): named after Raby Castle, Co. Durham.

Alnwick Castle (Saville Street, North Shields): named after Alnwick Castle, Northumberland.

Ballarat (Saville Street West, North Shields): named after the Ballarat Goldfields, Australia.

Fire Station (York Road, Whitley Bay): standing on the site of the old fire station.

Puns and Corruptions

Although puns became increasingly popular through the twentieth century, they should be considered with care. Supposed corruptions of foreign phrases usually have much simpler explanations, and many newer public houses have catchy names which are nothing other than a modern marketing strategy, such as **The Furry Pear** (The Arcade, Tynemouth) or **The Magic Lantern** (Preston North Road, North Shields).

Bell and Bucket (Norfolk Street, North Shields): a pun based on the fact that the pub stands on the site of the old North Shields fire station.

Sailors Return (Bell Street, North Shields): an old name based on the riverside area of North Shields and the many sailors who frequented the town.

Uncle Tom's Cabin (Bedford Street, North Shields): an amusing name taken from a book written by Harriet Beecher Stowe in 1852.

Flower Pot (Albion Road West): a name taken from its original connection with the plants, flowers and extensive gardens at one time associated with the pub.

The Bedroom (Whitley Road, Whitley Bay): modern marketing for a theme pub.

Sammy Jacks (Front Street, Tynemouth): modern marketing.

Religious

Public houses sometimes took their names from religious symbolism, such as **The Anchor** (Swans Quay/Duke Street and Bell Street, North Shields), taken from the Bible passage (Hebrews 6:19): 'We have this as a sure and steadfast anchor of the soul, a hope'. This also relates to the derivation of the name **Hope & Anchor**.

Lamb (Dotwick Street, North Shields): from John 1:29: 'Behold the Lamb of God, which taketh away the sins of the world'.

Salutation (Bell Street, North Shields and Front Street, Tynemouth): the salute (by handshake) of the Archangel Gabriel to Mary when informing her she was to carry Jesus Christ.

Royalty

Royal names have always been popular (except under Oliver Cromwell's rule). It demonstrated the landlord's loyalty to authority (whether he was loyal or not) especially after the Restoration of the Monarchy when Richard Cromwell (Oliver's son) was sacked and Charles II was brought back from exile.

North Shields and the surrounding environs had their share of public houses that were named after members of the monarchy, and other items of royal symbolism. Perhaps one of the most popular 'royal' pub names in the United Kingdom is the 'Queen Victoria', named after the queen who was the monarch at the time of greatest expansion of housing stock and associated public houses. She inspired great loyalty and affection, and publicans aimed to reflect this.

Examples of 'royal' pub names in the North Shields and surrounding areas are the **Kings Arms**, the **Kings Head, Queens Head**, **Crown & Sceptre**, **Victoria** and **William IV**, etc.

Ships

A pub name is sometimes taken from the name of a ship, such as the **Ship Hopewell** (Duke Street, North Shields), the **Ship Lady Jane** (Bell Street), or the **Royal Sovereign** (Bath Terrace, Tynemouth).

Trades and Tools

Many of the trade-related names could also be derived from a heraldry source, such as the **Carpenters Arms** (Clive Street), **Cordwainers Arms** (Bell Street), **Masons Arms** (Ropery Bank, Stephenson Street and Bedford Street, North Shields), **Shipwrights Arms** (Bell Street, Clive Street and Church Way, North Shields and Back Street, Tynemouth), **Shepherdess** (Bell Street), **Post Boy** (Stephenson Street, North Shields) and **Plough** (Dotwick Street, North Shields and Earsdon).

Transport

Rail: The Station, The Railway, The Express. (Usually pubs found close to a railway line or station).

Road: Waggon Inn, Coach & Horses, Pack Horse.

Water: Ferry, Ship, Brig, Corvette, Seine Boat, Navigation Tavern.

Trade Guilds

It is worth noting that some names starting with the word 'Three' are usually based on the arms of the London livery companies or trade guilds, such as the **Three Horseshoes** (Chapel Lane, Monkseaton), **The Farriers**, **Three Tuns** (Wooden Bridge, North Shields), the **Brewers and Vinters**.

Chapter One
North Shields Low Town

ABERDEEN ARMS, CLIVE STREET
First recorded in 1893; last recorded in 1908.

ADMIRAL JERVIS, NO. 73 BELL STREET
First recorded in 1857; last recorded in 1887.
The Admiral Jervis is shown under this name on a map dated 1857: however, it was later to become known as the Sun Inn, and was a larger pub situated on the south side of Bell Street, standing opposite the foot of Fenwicks Bank Stairs, backing onto the river Tyne. The pub was no doubt named after Admiral Sir John Jervis, who served alongside Captain James Cook and General Wolfe at the siege of Quebec in 1759. In the French Wars, Jervis commanded the Mediterranean and Channel Fleets. He was known as a stern disciplinarian with a grim sense of humour. Admiral Jervis took command of the fleet at a time when, in his own words, 'it was at the lowest ebb of licentiousness and ill discipline'. Through his own ruthless determination he transformed the fleet into a highly efficient fighting service.

ADMIRAL NELSON, 29/49 LIDDELL STREET
First recorded in 1822; last recorded in 1901.
Also known as the Lord Nelson, this building was situated on the bank side of Liddell Street, opposite the present Prince of Wales Tavern. The pub closed in 1901.

ANCHOR TAVERN, SWAN'S QUAY AND CLIVE STREET AND 18 DUKE STREET
First recorded in 1834; last recorded in 1897.
Also referred to as the Foul Anchor and the Raffled Anchor, this tavern was situated on Swan's Quay, (between Clive Street and the river Tyne), adjacent to the very narrow Hole-in-the-Wall Quay at the rear. The anchor has obvious connections with the shipping in a busy North Shields riverside port: however, the origins were probably derived from religious symbolism, after the Bible passage (Hebrews 6:19): 'Which Hope we have as an Anchor of the soul, both sure and stedfast, and which entereth into that within the veil'.

BACKWORTH ARMS, LIDDELL STREET
First recorded in 1892; last recorded in 1906.

BARLEY MOW, CLIVE STREET (EXACT LOCATION UNCONFIRMED)
First recorded in 1827; last recorded in 1827.
The Barley Mow is not an uncommon name for a public house, and the name is derived from part of the brewing process. Barley is laid in a malting, heated and watered until the grain germinates.

The large building in the centre of the picture is the derelict Black Swan Inn, *c.* 1910.

The grain is then cooked which kills the germination process and the result is called malt. Malt is the ingredient in beer which gives it its sweet taste and colour. The mow is a stack.

BAY HORSE, CLIVE STREET AND BAY HORSE QUAY
First recorded in 1822; last recorded in 1887.
The Bay Horse was situated just off Clive Street, near the end of Bay Horse Quay, and backed directly onto the river Tyne.

BIRD, CLIVE STREET
First recorded in 1847; last recorded in 1847.

BLACK BOY, CLIVE STREET
First recorded in 1834; last recorded in 1834.

BLACK BULL INN (REFER TO: GREEN MAN), 14/15/22 LIDDELL STREET AND PANDON BANK

BLACK COCK, CLIVE STREET AND BLACK COCK QUAY
First recorded in 1822; last recorded in 1834.

BLACK LION, 5/38/40 CLIVE STREET AND STEAM MILL LANE
First recorded in 1822; last recorded in 1964.
Situated directly opposite Britannia Bank Stairs, to the east side of Clive Street, the Black Lion, (sometimes referred to as the Old Black Lion), stood on the northern corner junction with Steam Mill Lane. An imposing four-storey Georgian-style structure, standing only a few yards away from the Golden Fleece, the building had a curved, recessed corner entrance, and two unusual decorative stone-faced circular windows to an upper storey. The Black Lion was adjoined to the Percy Arms, which stood on Steam Mill Lane, the cobbles of which are still evident behind the Golden Fleece.

Having existed since at least 1850, the Black Lion was still open in 1964, before being demolished in 1967 to make way for a new building, which was to become the North Eastern Rubber Co.

BLACK SWAN INN, 93 BELL STREET AND BLAND SQUARE
First recorded in 1690; last recorded in 1903.

The Black Swan Inn, situated on the south side of Bell Street, extended southwards towards the river Tyne. The premises had an extensive frontage of about 65ft, with a timber-built gallery beyond, and a river frontage of about 40ft, and the west side of the building overlooked Bland Square. It was first mentioned in an abstract of deeds dated February 1690. The basement comprised two vaulted cellars under the bar, with a large ceiled cellar extending towards the river. The ground floor consisted of a large bar, sitting room, snug, club room (with a gallery outside overlooking the river), kitchen and W.C. On the first floor, there were three bedrooms, a sitting room, bathroom and numerous large closets, with twelve other large rooms within the property. A further gallery was used in connection with the cellarage, fitted with a crane, which was able to lift up to a ton in weight. Access to the Black Swan from the river was via a passage to the left of the building, next to Lambs Quay, and Maitlands Lane, which is to the right of the picture, gave access to Bell Street.

BLACKSMITHS ARMS, 34 LIDDELL STREET
First recorded in 1886; last recorded in 1886.

BLUE BELL, 46 BELL STREET
First recorded in 1855; last recorded in 1930.

The Blue Bell was one of the larger public houses on Bell Street, and it was situated on the north side of the road, immediately next to the foot of the High Lighthouse Stairs.

BLYTH HOUSE, CLIVE STREET
First recorded in unconfirmed; last recorded in unconfirmed.

Facing Clive Street, from the east side of the road, the Blyth House was situated between Scarp Landing and Skipsey's Quay.

BOARD INN, 17 LIDDELL STREET AND CLIVE STREET
First recorded in 1834; last recorded in 1834.

The Board Inn was probably the smallest of all the inns and taverns in North Shields Low Town. It stood on the west side of Clive Street opposite the Star and Garter Inn, where Wascoe's Bank Stairs separated it from the Londonderry Arms, which stood next door to the south.

BOARS HEAD, CLIVE STREET AND BROAD QUAY
First recorded in 1822; last recorded in 1834.

BRITANNIA, CLIVE STREET
First recorded in 1822; last recorded in 1834.

BURNS' TAVERN, CLIVE STREET AND BELL STREET, CUSTOM HOUSE QUAY AND BROAD QUAY
First recorded in 1822; last recorded in 1899.

Collectively known as Burns' Tavern, the Burns Head, the Robert Burns and Robbie Burns Inn were named after the famous Scottish poet (1759-1796). This inn was hidden away from view, and situated between Broad Quay and Skipsey's Quay, at the eastern end of Clive Street, near Wooden Bridge. The back of the building faced the river Tyne.

CARPENTERS ARMS, CLIVE STREET AND SKIPP'S QUAY
First recorded in 1822; last recorded in 1827.

COBLE INN, 19/33 BELL STREET AND COBLE ENTRY
First recorded in 1834; last recorded in 1899.
The Coble Inn, or Coble Boat as it was sometimes known, was situated on the northern side of Bell Street next to Coble Entry, which led up the bankside to Tyne Street via Ropery Lane and Ropery Stairs.

COCK TAVERN, 27 CLIVE STREET
First recorded in 1822; last recorded in 1850.
Early origins of this pub name probably had a connection with the bloodthirsty sport of cockfighting.

COLLINGWOOD TAVERN, 1 BELL STREET
First recorded in 1847; last recorded in 1847.

CORDWAINERS ARMS, BELL STREET
First recorded in 1822; last recorded in 1827.
The term Cordwainer has generally fallen out of use from the English language. A cordwainer (or cordovan) is somebody who makes shoes and other articles from fine soft leather. The word is derived from 'cordwain', or 'cordovan', the leather produced in Cordoba, Spain. It is open to speculation why the Cordwainers Arms was so named.

CROWN INN, 30 CLIVE STREET
First recorded in 1850; last recorded in 1855.
The Crown Inn stood on the west side of Clive Street, adjacent to the New Quay Stairs, opposite the present Golden Fleece pub. The Crown was demolished in the late 1800s to make way for St Peter's Church which was built on the corner of Clive Street and Borough Road Bank.

CROWN AND ANCHOR, CLIVE STREET
First recorded in 1855; last recorded in 1855.
Situated on the east side of Clive Street, the Crown and Anchor adjoined the Hole in the Wall Quay to the north.

CROWN AND CUSHION, 44 LIDDELL STREET
First recorded in 1850; last recorded in 1865.
The Crown and Cushion was situated on the south side of Liddell Street, directly opposite the Green Man (Black Bull Inn) and the foot of Green Man Bank.

CUMBERLAND ARMS, 27/40 LIDDELL STREET
First recorded in 1850; last recorded in 1865.
The Cumberland Arms or Cumberland House as it was also known, stood on the south side of Liddell Street, opposite the bottom of Pandon Bank. The inn adjoined the Trawlers Arms.

CUMBERLAND ARMS, LOW LIGHTS
First recorded in 1865; last recorded in 1865.

CUSTOM HOUSE TAVERN, BELL STREET AND UNION QUAY
First recorded in 1850; last recorded in 1865.
The Custom House Tavern was a small building which stood on the south side of the road, at the eastern end of Bell Street, directly next to Union Quay.

CYPRUS, 24 CLIVE STREET
First recorded in 1887; last recorded in 1899.
The Cyprus Inn was one of the very small Low Town Inns, and stood on the east side of Clive Street, between Swan's Quay and Steel's Quay.

DOCK HOUSE, 16/23/42 LIDDELL STREET
First recorded in 1822; last recorded in 1899.
The Dock House, also known as the Dock Hotel, was only a small pub, which was situated at the commencement of the narrowest part of the road on the south side of Liddell Street. The pub was the neighbour of the Trawlers Arms next door, with the larger Green Man (Black Bull Inn) opposite.

DUNDEE ARMS, UNION ROAD
First recorded in 1834; last recorded in 1834.

DUTALIA HOTEL, CLIVE STREET AND STEEL'S QUAY
First recorded in unconfirmed; last recorded in unconfirmed.
Situated off Clive Street to the east, the Dutalia Hotel overlooked the river Tyne on Steel's Quay, adjoining the Lindsay Arms. The origin of the name 'Dutalia' has not been ascertained.

EAGLE TAVERN, BLAND SQUARE
First recorded in 1847; last recorded in 1847.

EAGLE, SKIPSEYS' QUAY
First recorded in 1850; last recorded in 1850.

EDINBURGH CASTLE, 80 CLIVE STREET
First recorded in 1822; last recorded in 1834.

EDINBURGH CASTLE, 26 BELL STREET
First recorded in 1855; last recorded in 1865.
The Edinburgh Castle stood towards the eastern end of Bell Street, at the foot of, and adjacent to Stewart's Bank Stairs.

ENGLISH AND FRENCH FLAG, BELL STREET AND BLAND SQUARE
First recorded in 1855; last recorded in 1855.
The reason for this unusual combination of names is unknown; however, it is likely to have been derived from the Napoleonic Wars. Exact location unconfirmed.

EUROPEAN, STEELS QUAY
First recorded in 1867; last recorded in 1867.

EXCHANGE VAULTS (REFER TO: WATERLOO INN), 31/51 CLIVE STREET
Also referred to as the Exchange Inn, the Exchange Vaults and the Exchange Hotel.

Looking north along Clive Street, just beyond the post office, the Exchange Inn (Exchange Hotel) can be seen standing on the inside of the curve of the road. *c.* 1930.

FLAG, BLAND'S SQUARE QUAY
First recorded in unconfirmed; last recorded in unconfirmed.
Early maps show The Flag as overlooking the river Tyne on Bland's Square Quay on part of the site also indicated as being occupied by the Black Swan Inn.

FREEMASONS ARMS, 3 BELL STREET
First recorded in 1850; last recorded in 1850.
The Freemasons Arms was located on Lamb Quay, and overlooked the river Tyne, at the rear of Bell Street. The larger Nag's Head adjoined this pub at the corner of Lamb Quay and Bell Street.

GEORGE IV, 91 BELL STREET
First recorded in 1833-1855 as George IV; last recorded in 1855-1861 as the Sailors Return.
The George IV public house was located on the south side of Bell Street, adjacent to Maitland's Lane, which led to Maitland's Quay. It was named after George IV, King of Great Britain and Ireland and of Hanover (1820–1830) who caused controversy when he attempted to divorce his estranged wife, Caroline of Brunswick. The pub was renamed the Sailors Return in 1855.

GEORGE IV, CLIVE STREET AND APPLEBYS BANK
First recorded in 1827; last recorded in 1827.

GLOBE INN, 20 CLIVE STREET
First recorded in 1855; last recorded in 1887.
The Globe Inn was situated on Clive Street, immediately next to the Hole in the Wall Quay to the south, and Bird in Hand Quay to the north. It was often referred to as the Marble Bar.

GLOBE, 56 BELL STREET
First recorded in 1822; last recorded in 1855.
The Globe stood towards the eastern end of Bell Street, near the foot of Fenwick's Bank Stairs.

GOLDEN EAGLE, UNION STREET
First recorded in 1822; last recorded in 1827.

GOLDEN LION INN, 12/35/36 UNION STREET AND CHURCH WAY
First recorded in 1822; last recorded in 1928.
Originally standing on the east side of Church Way, the Golden Lion was extended in the later part of the 1800s to incorporate the building on the northern corner of Union Street to become a corner site. The inn stood directly opposite the Prince of Wales, near to the top of Causey Bank.

GOLDEN LION, CLIVE STREET
First recorded in 1822; last recorded in 1834.

GREEN MAN, 14/15/22 LIDDELL STREET AND PANDON BANK
First recorded in 1822 as the Green Man; last recorded in 1899 as the Black Bull Inn.
The unusually named Green Man was a large building which stood at the commencement of the narrowest part of Liddell Street, adjacent to the steep stairs of Green Man Bank (Pandon Bank Stairs). It was situated on the north side of the road directly opposite the Crown and Cushion, the Dock Hotel and the Trawlers Arms. The original images of a Green Man are often found in churches as a face peering through leaves and petals; this character is the Will o' the Wisp. Some pub signs will also show the Green Man as he appears in English traditional sword dances (in green tats). The Green Man may also be linked to the legend of Robin Hood. The Green Man was later renamed the Black Bull Inn.

GREY HORSE (REFER TO: GRIDIRON HOUSE), 55 BELL STREET AND GREY HORSE QUAY

GREYHOUND, BELL STREET
First recorded in 1834; last recorded in 1834.

GRIDIRON HOUSE, 55 BELL STREET
First recorded in 1847 as the Gridiron House; recorded in 1850 as the Low Grey Horse; last recorded in 1855 as the Grey Horse.

HALF MOON INN, LOW LIGHTS AND BACK UNION ROAD
First recorded in 1822; last recorded in 1940.
The Half Moon Inn was one of the many buildings forming the area around the Low Lights. It was located to the east of and behind Union Road near to Clifford's Fort. The neighbouring Waggon Inn stood on Union Road, slightly offset to the rear of the Half Moon.

HARTLEY HOUSE, SHEPHERD'S QUAY
First recorded in 1834; last recorded in 1834.

HIBERNIAN TAVERN, BELL STREET
First recorded in 1855; last recorded in 1855.
'Hibernia' is the Latin and poetic name for the island of Ireland, so there may well have been an Irish connection when this pub was so named. Its exact location is unconfirmed.

HIGHLANDER, 41 LIDDELL STREET, UNION ROAD AND UNION QUAY
First recorded in 1834; last recorded in 1930.
Sometimes referred to as the Old Highlander, this pub was rebuilt on the site of an earlier pub of the same name. The Highlander was a large inn which faced the river Tyne on the north side of Union Quay. The building stood close to the Newcastle Arms and the Lord Collingwood, and slightly to the east of the foot of Naters Bank Stairs. The actual building still exists today as William Wight's Grocers Store.

HOPE AND ANCHOR, LOW LIGHTS AND BACK UNION ROAD
First recorded in 1822; last recorded in 1855.
The Hope and Anchor was a very small inn, and part of the area known as the Low Lights. It was situated to the east of and behind Union Road near Clifford's Fort. The neighbouring Queens Head stood directly next door to it.

HOPE AND ANCHOR, 16/28 BELL STREET
First recorded in 1822; last recorded in 1887.
The Hope and Anchor stood on the north side of Bell Street, at the foot of Turpin's Bank Stairs.

JERUSALEM COFFEE HOUSE, CLIVE STREET
First recorded in 1822; last recorded in 1855.
Situated to the east side of Clive Street, the unusually named Jerusalem Coffee House was tucked away overlooking the river, behind the Kings Head public house, on the Jerusalem Coffee House Quay.

JOLLY SAILOR, CLIVE STREET AND BIRD-IN-HAND QUAY
First recorded in 1850; last recorded in 1850.

KINGS ARMS, 62 CLIVE STREET
First recorded in 1822; last recorded in 1850.
The Kings Arms is a common name for pubs both in England and elsewhere. The name refers to the coat of arms of a king, which a pub of this name would display prominently above its door as a means of identifying it.

KINGS HEAD, CLIVE STREET AND JERUSALEM COFFEE HOUSE QUAY
First recorded in 1822; last recorded in 1887.
Situated to the east side of Clive Street, the Kings Head adjoined the Jerusalem Coffee House on the Jerusalem Coffee House Quay.

KINGS HEAD, UNION STREET
First recorded in 1822; last recorded in 1822.

KIRKCALDY ARMS (REFER TO: OLD LIGHTHOUSE), 35 BELL STREET

LAMB, 21/23 BELL STREET AND BLAND SQUARE
First recorded in 1822; last recorded in 1850.
This name could well have been adopted from religious symbolism, taken from John 1:29: 'Behold the Lamb of God, which taketh away the sins of the world'.

LASS O' GOWRIE, CLIVE STREET
First recorded in 1850; last recorded in 1850.
'The Lass O'Gowrie' was a poem written by Lady Carolina Nairne (1766-1845), a Scottish poet who

Kirkcaldy Arms, *c.* 1906.

was well known during her lifetime. Most of her work was published under a pseudonym. Gowrie is an area of farm belt famous for its fruit in Perth and Kinross, central Scotland, along the northern shore of the Firth of Tay, between Perth and Dundee. The pub was no doubt named as a tribute to the poem.

LINDSAY ARMS, 25/26 CLIVE STREET
First recorded in 1865; last recorded in 1887.
The Lindsay Arms stood on the east side of Clive Street, separated from the Star and Garter Inn by the alleyway leading to Steel's Quay. To the rear, the lesser known Dutalia Hotel adjoined it and backed onto the river Tyne.

LOMBARD ARMS, 15 CLIVE STREET AND LISHMAN'S QUAY
First recorded in 1855; last recorded in 1887.
The Lombard Arms stood on the east side of Clive Street, opposite the foot of Barnes' Bank, next to Lishman's Quay.

LONDONDERRY ARMS, CLIVE STREET
First recorded in 1855; last recorded in 1855.
The Londonderry Arms stood on the west side of Clive Street opposite the Star and Garter Inn. Wascoe's Bank Stairs separated it from the Board Inn, which stood next door.

LORD COLLINGWOOD, 10 UNION QUAY, UNION ROW AND UNION ROAD
First recorded in 1822; last recorded in 1930.
The Lord Collingwood stood at the foot of Naters Bank Stairs, and faced the river Tyne on the north side of Union Quay. The building was situated directly next door to the Newcastle Arms, the site of which is now that of the Fishermen's Mission.

Low Lights Tavern, 1983.

LORD CORNWALLIS, CLIVE STREET
First recorded in 1822; last recorded in 1827.
This public house was probably named in honour of Charles Cornwallis, 1st Marquis and 2nd Earl Cornwallis (1738–1805). He was a British military and political leader who commanded forces in North Carolina during the American Revolution. His surrender at Yorktown in 1781 marked the final British defeat.

LOW LIGHTS TAVERN, 8 BREWHOUSE BANK AND LOW LIGHTS
First recorded in 1834; last recorded in 2007.
Believed to have been an alehouse for over 400 years, the Low Lights Tavern is situated on the east side of Brewhouse Bank not far from the Low Lights area. It is one of the oldest surviving taverns still standing in the former 'Low Town' of North Shields, and retains a typical charm and character that it probably possessed when it was first built. In the 1800s the Low Lights Brewery and Maltings formed the adjoining buildings, hence the name of Brewhouse or Brewery Bank.

LOYAL STANDARD, BELL STREET
First recorded in 1822; last recorded in 1834.

LUCKY BOB, CLIVE STREET
First recorded in 1851; last recorded in 1851.

LUMPERS ARMS, 15 CLIVE STREET AND LISHMAN'S QUAY
First recorded in 1855; last recorded in 1887.
The Lumpers Arms stood towards the east side of Clive Street, adjacent to Lishman's Quay, and overlooked the river to the rear. By 1896, it was replaced by the Lombard Arms, situated next door on Clive Street.

MARINERS ARMS, 28 BELL STREET
First recorded in 1834; last recorded in 1834.

MASONS ARMS, ROPERY BANK
First recorded in 1822; last recorded in 1899.
As well as the Freemasons symbol of the square and compass inscribed within three circles, the Mason's Arms also bore upon its sign the words 'Ship in Launch', a name by which the pub was also known. Why this particular sign was there, or what the words meant, no one knew. Had it been the 'Ship Inn Launch' or the 'Ship Launch Inn', the meaning might have been easier to understand; however, the name 'Ship in Launch' still remains a mystery. The premises were small, almost hidden from sight behind a number of buildings situated near to the foot of Tanners Bank, between Union Road and the river Tyne.

NAGS HEAD, 98 BELL STREET
First recorded in 1855; last recorded in 1865.
The Nags Head stood on the south side of Bell Street, at the corner with Lamb Quay to the east. Adjoining the pub to the rear was the Freemasons Arms, which overlooked the river Tyne.

NAVAL RESERVE, 11 BELL STREET
First recorded in 1887; last recorded in 1887.

NEPTUNE, CLIVE STREET
First recorded in 1850; last recorded in 1850.

NEW DOLPHIN INN (REFER TO: STAITH HOUSE), 57 LOW LIGHTS AND UNION ROAD

NEWCASTLE ARMS, 10 CLIVE STREET
First recorded in 1822; last recorded in 1855.
Situated about 100 yards from the corner of Borough Road Bank, the Newcastle Arms stood on the west side of Clive Street opposite the entrance to Elders Quay.

NEWCASTLE ARMS, 11 UNION QUAY AND LOW LIGHTS
First recorded in 1822; last recorded in 1930.
The Newcastle Arms faced the river Tyne on the north side of Union Quay. The building was situated directly next door to the Lord Collingwood. The site is now occupied by the Fishermen's Mission House.

NORTH STAR (REFER TO: OLD LIGHTHOUSE), 35/36 BELL STREET

NORTHUMBERLAND INN, CLIVE STREET
First recorded in 1851; last recorded in 1851.

OLD LIGHTHOUSE, 35/36 BELL STREET
First recorded in 1822-1855 as the Old Lighthouse; 1855-1887 as the North Star; last recorded in 1887-1907 as the Kirkcaldy Arms.
This building probably dates back to Elizabethan days, and as the name suggests, the Old Lighthouse probably derived its name from the High Lighthouse which stood on Tyne Street, at the top of the bank above Bell Street. It later became the North Star, then the Kirkcaldy Arms before closure as a pub in 1907, when it became a butcher's shop and then a grocer's. It has been long since demolished.

A trio of pubs is shown in this early 1900s view of Union Quay. The Newcastle Arms, the Lord Collingwood and The Highlander are clearly visible here. The large white building in the middle of the picture is The Highlander, which was separated from the Lord Collingwood by Naters Bank Stairs.

ORDNANCE ARMS, LOW LIGHTS
First recorded in 1822; last recorded in 1827.
As this building stood in the area known as the Low Lights, close to Clifford's Fort, it is probable that the early association with the fort resulted in the name to the pub.

PACK HORSE, CLIVE STREET
First recorded in 1850; last recorded in 1850.

PERCY ARMS, CLIVE STREET AND STEAM MILL LANE
First recorded in 1850; last recorded in 1855.
Situated opposite Britannia Bank Stairs, to the east side of Clive Street, the Percy Arms adjoined the Old Black Lion, which stood at the corner of Steam Mill Lane, and Clive Street behind the Golden Fleece. The building has long since been demolished and the site was later occupied by the North Eastern Rubber Co.

PHOENIX, CLIVE STREET
First recorded in 1822; last recorded in 1834.

Looking east along Liddell Street, the Prince of Wales and the Wooden Doll are depicted in the photograph, and the neighbouring pub which stood next door, separated by Seven Stars Quay, was called 'the Seven Stars', and is visible at the end of the building line, where Liddle Street became Bell Street. Another public house which stood almost opposite the Prince of Wales was the Admiral Nelson, the small bay window of which is just visible on the left of the photograph.

POLKA, 11 BELL STREET
First recorded in 1865; last recorded in 1865.
The Polka is a lively dance which originated in Bohemia, and there is no obvious connection, or reason why this pub was so named.

PORTER VAT, ROPERY BANK AND ROPERY WALK
First recorded in: not recorded; last recorded: not recorded.

PRINCE COBURG, CLIVE STREET AND BIRD-IN-HAND QUAY
First recorded in 1822; last recorded in 1834.
The name Coburg originated from Queen Victoria's connection with Prince Albert who descended from the German house of Saxe-Coburg and Gotha.

PRINCE OF PRUSSIA, 7 CLIVE STREET
First recorded in 1865; last recorded in 1865.
It is likely that this pub was named in honour of Prince Heinrich of Prussia, who was born in 1862 and was the third of eight children born to Crown Prince Friedrich III (later Emperor Friedrich III), and Victoria, Princess Royal of Great Britain, a daughter of the British Queen Victoria.

PRINCE OF WALES TAVERN, 31/32 LIDDELL STREET, BELL STREET AND CUSTOM
HOUSE QUAY
First recorded in 1850; last recorded in 2007.
This building is one of the oldest public houses still operating in North Shields, and records indicate
that a pub has stood on this site since the early 1600s. The Prince of Wales was at one time one of the
largest taverns in the Low Town, and occupied a site on what was then a very narrow Liddell Street.
It was originally nicknamed 'The Old Wooden Doll', because of the famous wooden dolly figurehead
associated with the North Shields fishing trade, which stood outside the premises in the adjacent
alleyway on Custom House Quay. There have been several wooden dollies at this location, the first of
which was erected in 1814 by Alexander Bartleman, a local ship owner and brewer.

It soon became a traditional custom for superstitious sailors to carve off a sliver of wood from the
figure, believing it would bring them good luck before they set off on a voyage – as a result of which,
it was completely destroyed within a few years, resulting in another one being made and erected in
1820 (which eventually suffered the same fate). In June 1864, a third wooden doll was made and set
in place beside the pub but in the late 1890s, it was broken in two, prompting calls for yet another
replacement. The fourth doll was made in 1902, a copy of which was placed in Northumberland
Square in 1958.

Following the decline of the fishing industry, the Prince of Wales closed for a number of years
during the mid 1970s until its acquisition by Sam Smith's Brewery, of Tadcaster, who reopened it in
1992 after carrying out an extensive refurbishment. The brewery arranged for a replacement copy of
the third wooden doll to be returned to its original site next to the pub.

Opposite: Still existing today on Liddell Street, the Prince of Wales has changed very little from this old 1930s view.

Right: Another early view of the Low Town, on Clive Street, with the sign for the Red Lamp Inn visible to the left.

PRINCE OF WALES, 7-8 UNION STREET AND CAUSEY BANK
First recorded in 1855; last recorded in 1940.
The Prince of Wales occupied a position to the east of Causey Bank, on the south side of Union Street, opposite the Golden Lion Inn.

PRINCE OF WALES' FEATHERS, 51 LIDDELL STREET
First recorded in 1855; last recorded in 1855.
Situated on Liddell Street, North Shields, this inn was later renamed the Princess of Wales.

PRINCESS OF WALES (REFER TO: PRINCE OF WALES' FEATHER), 51 LIDDELL STREET

PUNCHEON, 39 UNION STREET
First recorded in 1865; last recorded in 1899 as the Rector House.
The Puncheon stood on the north side of Union Street, between Church Way and Bedford Street, and probably took its name from a puncheon, which is an old word, referring to a cask with a capacity of between 70 and 120 gallons. Prior to 1887, the name was changed to the Rector House.

QUEENS HEAD, FERRY BOAT LANDING
First recorded in 1834; last recorded in 1834.

North Shields Ferry Landing, *c.* 1920.

QUEENS HEAD, LOW LIGHTS AND BACK UNION ROAD
First recorded in 1855; last recorded in 1887.
The Queens Head was a very small inn, and part of the area known as the Low Lights. It was situated to the east of, and behind Union Road near Clifford's Fort. The neighbouring Hope and Anchor stood directly next door to it

RAILWAY TAVERN, 57 CLIVE STREET
First recorded in: not recorded; last recorded in: not recorded.
An unusual name for a tavern in this part of North Shields, as there is no obvious connection with a railway in this area.

RECTOR HOUSE (REFER TO: PUNCHEON), 39 UNION STREET

RED LAMP INN, 57 CLIVE STREET AND RATCLIFF'S BANK
First recorded in 1887; last recorded in 1930.
The Red Lamp Inn was situated on the west side of Clive Street, adjacent to the south side of Ratcliff's Bank Stairs.

ROB ROY, CLIVE STREET
First recorded in 1855; last recorded in 1855.
Named after the Scottish clan leader and outlaw whose banditry is the subject of Sir Walter Scott's novel *Rob Roy* in 1817.

ROBERT BURNS TAVERN (REFER TO: BURNS TAVERN), CLIVE STREET AND BROAD QUAY

ROEBUCK, LIDDELL STREET
First recorded in 1822; last recorded in 1827.
A roebuck, being a male roe deer, is an unusual name for a pub located near North Shields riverside.

ROSE AND CROWN, LIDDELL STREET
First recorded in 1822; last recorded in 1834.
After the Battle of Bosworth Field in which King Richard III was killed, the victor Henry Tudor proclaimed himself King Henry VII. Henry had no real claim to the throne of England, so had to legitimise his position: this he did by marrying someone who did have a claim – Princess Elizabeth of York. She was so beautiful she was known as the Rose of York, hence the commemorating pub name: the Rose is Princess Elizabeth, and the Crown is Henry VII.

ROSE OF ALLENDALE, 24 BELL STREET
First recorded in 1865; last recorded in 1865.

ROYAL OAK, 61 BELL STREET
First recorded in 1822; last recorded in 1887.
The Royal Oak stood on the south side of Bell Street, opposite the foot of Lighthouse Bank, and backed directly onto the river Tyne at Dawson's Quay. After the Battle of Worcester in 1651, during the English Civil War, the defeated Prince Charles escaped the scene with the Roundheads on his tail. He managed to reach Shifnal in Shropshire, where he found an oak tree (now know as the Boscobel Oak). He climbed the tree and hid in it for a day while the obviously short-sighted Parliamentarians strolled around under the tree looking for him. After the hunters gave up, Prince Charles came down and escaped to France. He became King Charles II on the Restoration of the Monarchy. To celebrate this good fortune, the 29 May (Charles' birthday) was declared Royal Oak Day and the pub's name commemorated this.

ROYAL STANDARD, CLIVE STREET AND SHEPHERD'S QUAY
First recorded in 1822; last recorded in 1827.

SAILORS RETURN (REFER TO: GEORGE IV), 45/91 BELL STREET AND SHEPHERD'S QUAY

SALUTATION, BELL STREET
First recorded in 1822; last recorded in 1822.
A salutation is any word or words used as a greeting; it was a popular choice of name for many English public houses.

SARACENS HEAD, LIDDELL STREET
First recorded in 1834; last recorded in 1834.
The Saracens Head was at one time a fairly common name for many public houses throughout the country. In older Western historical literature, the Saracens were the people of the Saracen Empire, another name for the Arab Caliphate under the rule of the Umayyad and Abbasid dynasties. The Saracens are credited with many mathematical advances and inventions used in the modern world.

The Seven Stars, Wooden Bridge, 1920.

SAWYERS ARMS, BELL STREET
First recorded in 1855; last recorded in 1855.
The Sawyers Arms was situated on the north side of Bell Street, adjoining the foot of King George Stairs, and diagonally opposite the Nag's Head.

SCOTCH ARMS, BROAD QUAY
First recorded in 1847; last recorded in 1847.

SEVEN STARS, 1 WOODEN BRIDGE
First recorded in 1822; last recorded in 1930.
The Seven Stars was located in the area known as Wooden Bridge, which is the road at the foot of Bedford Street where it forms the junction with Liddell Street. Effectively, when travelling from west to east, the Seven Stars is the first of all the pubs on the north side of Liddell Street.

SEVEN STARS, 1/89/109 BELL STREET, LIDDELL STREET AND SEVEN STARS QUAY
First recorded in 1822; last recorded in 1899.
The Seven Stars on Bell Street had the same name as a neighbouring pub, just a few hundred yards away on Wooden Bridge, and confusion between the two must have been commonplace. This pub however, was situated on the south side of the road, directly next door to the Prince of Wales Tavern, and adjacent to Seven Stars Quay.

SHAKESPEARE INN, 17/31/33 CLIVE STREET AND SHEPHERD'S QUAY
First recorded in 1822; last recorded in 1897.
The Shakespeare Inn, or the Old Shakespeare Tavern, was a corner building, standing almost opposite the Exchange Inn, and situated on the east side of Clive Street to the north side of its junction with Shepherd's Quay. It stood just a few feet away from the Victoria Inn, located on the opposite corner of Shepherd's Quay and Clive Street.

SHAKESPEARE, LISHMAN'S QUAY
First recorded in 1834; last recorded in 1850.
William Shakespeare (1564-1616) was an English poet and playwright who had a number of inns named after him throughout the country.

SHEPHERDESS INN, 102 BELL STREET, ANCHOR QUAY AND SHEPHERDESS QUAY
First recorded in 1822; last recorded in 1899.
The Shepherdess Inn stood on the south side of Bell Street, backing on to the river Tyne and Anchor Quay.

SHIP INN, STEEL'S QUAY
First recorded in 1834; last recorded in 1850.

SHIP, 64/65/78/80 BELL STREET
First recorded in 1822; last recorded in 1899.
The Ship Inn stood on the south side of Bell Street, opposite to, and not far from the bottom of the High Lighthouse stairs. The inn backed onto the river Tyne between Mathwin's Quay and Dawson's Quay.

SHIP, CLIVE STREET AND SHEPHERD'S QUAY
First recorded in 1822; last recorded in 1827.

SHIP TAVERN, 14 CLIVE STREET
First recorded in 1822; last recorded in 1834.
The Ship stood on the western side of Clive Street, adjacent with Dawson's Bank to the north of the building.

SHIP AND WHALE, 20 BELL STREET
First recorded in 1822; last recorded in 1855.

SHIP LADY JANE, BELL STREET
First recorded in 1834; last recorded in 1834.
The suggestion is that this pub name was derived from a ship or vessel called *Lady Jane*, and probably named after Lady Jane Grey (1537-1554), a great-granddaughter of Henry VII of England, who reigned as uncrowned queen regnant of the kingdom of England for nine days in 1553.

SHIP IN LAUNCH (REFER TO: MASONS ARMS), LOW LIGHTS AND BACK UNION ROAD, TANNERS BANK

SHIPWRIGHTS ARMS, CLIVE STREET AND BELL STREET
First recorded in 1822; last recorded in 1827.

SHOULDER OF MUTTON, CLIVE STREET AND FERRY BOAT LANDING
First recorded in 1822; last recorded in 1850.

SIR WILLIAM WALLACE, CLIVE STREET
First recorded in 1855; last recorded in 1855.
This pub was named after William Wallace, who was one of Scotland's greatest national heroes and the undisputed leader of the Scottish resistance forces during the first years of the long but ultimately successful struggle to free Scotland from English rule at the end of the thirteenth century. He was knighted in December 1297 and proclaimed guardian of the kingdom.

STAITH HOUSE, 57 LOW LIGHTS AND UNION ROAD
First recorded in 1850 as the Staith House; last recorded in 2007 as the New Dolphin.
Situated opposite the foot of Brewhouse Bank, and to the east of Union Road near Clifford's Fort, the Staith House stood in the area known as the Low Lights. It was renamed as the New Dolphin prior to 1865. The inn is typically a fisherman's pub which has been modernised and extended over the years, and still exists to this day.

STAR AND GARTER, 26/28 CLIVE STREET AND STAR AND GARTER QUAY
First recorded in 1822; last recorded in 1899.
The Star and Garter (also known as the Star Inn), was one of the larger Low Town inns, which was situated on the east side of Clive Street, opposite the foot of Wascoe's Bank Stairs and next door to the Lindsay Arms. The pub is believed to date back as far as the Tudor period and existed into the 1920s. The length of the building ran adjacent to the Star and Garter Quay with the rear edge of the building overlooking the river Tyne.

STEAM MILL INN, CLIVE STREET, BLACK LION QUAY AND STEAM MILL LANE
First recorded in 1822; last recorded in 1834.

STONE HOUSE INN, 12 CLIVE STREET AND BLACK COCK QUAY
First recorded in 1855; last recorded in 1899.
The Stone House Inn was situated on the east side of Clive Street, almost opposite the foot of Linskill's Bank Stairs, between Black Cock Quay and Jerusalem Coffee House Quay.

SUN INN (REFER TO: ADMIRAL JERVIS), 73 BELL STREET

SUNDERLAND BRIDGE, 9 CLIVE STREET
First recorded in 1822; last recorded in 1887.
The Sunderland Bridge was a small inn, located on the east side of Clive Street and backing on to Black Cock Quay. It occupied a site on the south corner of the narrow passageway leading to Scarp Landing.

SUSPENSION BRIDGE, CLIVE STREET AND 4 BEDFORD STREET
First recorded in 1822; last recorded in 1834.

SWAN, CLIVE STREET
First recorded in 1822; last recorded in 1822.

SWEDISH ARMS, BELL STREET
First recorded in 1855; last recorded in 1855.

THREE BULL'S HEADS, UNION ROAD, UNION STREET AND LOW LIGHTS
First recorded in 1822; last recorded in 1834.

THREE TUNS, 4 WOODEN BRIDGE
First recorded in 1822; last recorded in 1865.
Near to the bottom of Bedford Street, just south of the Tiger Stairs and directly opposite the foot of Church Stairs, the Three Tuns was the neighbouring pub to the Tiger Inn. A tun is a large cask for liquids, especially wine, or a mash tun is an insulated vessel with a false bottom used in brewing. The three tuns are based on the arms of both the Worshipful Company of Vinters and the Worshipful Company of Brewers (City of London Guilds).

TRAVELLERS REST, 9 LIDDELL STREET
First recorded in 1865; last recorded in 1865.

TRAWLERS ARMS, LIDDELL STREET
First recorded: unconfirmed; last recorded: unconfirmed.
The Trawlers Arms was a small pub, situated on the south side of Liddell Street. It stood directly next door to the Dock Hotel, and directly opposite the much larger Black Bull Inn. The name had an obvious connection with the then busy fishing port of North Shields.

TYNE HOTEL, 19 CLIVE STREET AND BIRD-IN-HAND QUAY
First recorded in 1887; last recorded in 1899.
The Tyne Hotel was situated on the east side of Clive Street, almost opposite the foot of Coulson's Bank Stairs, and adjacent to the Bird in Hand Quay.

UNION TAVERN, 37 LIDDELL STREET AND DOCK QUAY
First recorded in 1822; last recorded in 1899.
One of the larger Low Town taverns, the Union Tavern was also known as the Union Inn or the Union Hotel, and stood directly opposite the foot of the Library Stairs, adjacent to Dock Quay, on the south side of Liddell Street.

VICTORIA INN, 32/34 CLIVE STREET AND SHEPHERD'S QUAY
First recorded in 1850; last recorded in 1899.
The Victoria Inn was a corner building, standing directly opposite the Exchange Inn, and situated on the east side of Clive Street to the south side of its junction with Shepherd's Quay. It stood just a few feet away from the Shakespeare Inn, located on the opposite corner of Shepherd's Quay and Clive Street.

VULCAN TAVERN, UNION ROAD
First recorded in 1834; last recorded in 1834.

WAGGON INN, 1 LOW LIGHTS AND UNION ROAD
First recorded in 1850; last recorded in 1930.
The Waggon Inn was one of a number of buildings forming the area around the Low Lights. It was situated on the east side of Union Road near to Clifford's Fort. The neighbouring Half Moon Inn stood behind it, and slightly offset from the rear of the Waggon.

The Albion Hotel was situated on Norfolk Street and faced west along Saville Street. It was demolished in 1884 allowing the road to be extended into Charlotte Street. The remainder of the building became better known as the Albion Grill, the large arched window of which is visible to the right.

WATERLOO INN, 16/31/51 CLIVE STREET
First recorded in 1850-1887 as the Waterloo Inn; last recorded in 1887-1938 as the Exchange Inn/Hotel.
Situated between Britannia Bank and Ratcliff's Bank Stairs, slightly to the north of the Newcastle Arms, the Waterloo Inn occupied a position on the west side of Clive Street, opposite the Victoria Inn, and Shepherd's Quay. Prior to 1887, the pub was renamed the Exchange Inn, or Exchange Vaults, and later as the Exchange Hotel.

WHEATSHEAF, 6 LIDDELL STREET
First recorded in 1822; last recorded in 1834.

WHITBY ARMS, 49 CLIVE STREET
First recorded in 1887; last recorded in 1887.

WHITE SWAN, LIDDELL STREET
First recorded in 1822; last recorded in 1834.

YARMOUTH ARMS, 65 BELL STREET
First recorded in 1850; last recorded in 1850.

Chapter Two
North Shields High Town

ADMIRAL NELSON, 69 GEORGE STREET
First recorded in 1895; last recorded in 1906.

ALBERT ARMS, 6 HOWARD STREET
First recorded in 1887; last recorded in 1912.
The Albert Arms was a small pub, near the foot of, and on the western side of Howard Street, just a few yards away from the Maritime Chambers Shipping Offices.

ALBERT INN, 18/19 ALBERT TERRACE AND 142 TYNEMOUTH ROAD
First recorded in 1887; last recorded in 2007.
The Albert Inn was situated on the corner of Albert Terrace, (Tynemouth Road) and North King Street. Albert Terrace is a sub-named street forming a short section of the North side of Tynemouth Road, between North Church Street and North King Street. The street and inn were probably named in honour of Queen Victoria's husband, Prince Albert.

ALBION HOTEL, 23 NORFOLK STREET AND 72 SAVILLE STREET
First recorded in 1850; last recorded in 1985.
The imposing Albion Hotel was one of the largest High Town buildings, and stood on Norfolk Street at the eastern end of Saville Street, facing west. The adjoining assembly rooms were founded in 1853 as part of the hotel. In 1884 the Albion Hotel was demolished, which allowed Saville Street to become a continuous thoroughfare and connect with Lower Pearson Street. This road later became known as Charlotte Street. The remaining Assembly Rooms were then remodelled to incorporate the Albion Hotel, on the corner site where it later became known as the Albion Grill. The premises closed down during the 1970s and were destroyed by a large fire in 1985. It was demolished shortly afterwards.

ALBION INN, 30 NILE STREET AND 17 ALBION ROAD
First recorded in 1887; last recorded in 2007.
The Albion Inn stands on the south-west corner of Albion Road and Nile Street. It was known locally as 'The Top House'.

ALNWICK CASTLE, 26/28 SAVILLE STREET AND 22/112 CHURCH WAY
First recorded in 1834-2005 as the Alnwick Castle; last recorded in 2005-2007 as the Teac Fiddlers.
The Alnwick Castle is one of the oldest established public houses still in existence in North Shields. The pub, which occupies a prominent site on the south side of Saville Street at the corner of Church Way, has barely been altered from its original shape, format and design. In January 2005, a part of

One of North Shields' more famous premises: the Alnwick Castle, *c.* 1948.

North Shields' heritage was lost when the famous and long-established name was changed to 'the Teac Fiddlers' as new owners took over to upgrade the image by converting the premises to an Irish style theme bar. A date which is incorporated into the Teac Fiddlers suggests it has existed since 1759. However, this is not really a date at all: it is in fact a play on numbers, being the time on the twenty-four-hour clock when the doors of the newly renamed pub were first opened to the public in 2005.

ANGEL HOTEL (REFER TO: VICTORIA HOTEL), ALBION STREET
First recorded in 1822-1897 as the Angel Hotel; last recorded in 1897-2007 as Ye Olde Hundred.
This pub was situated next door to the Victoria Hotel, and just prior to 1897, the two buildings were combined to become Ye Old Hundred.

AQUATIC ARMS, 1 WILLIAM STREET AND 76 RUDYERD STREET
First recorded in 1864; last recorded in the 1970s.
The Aquatic Arms was situated on the corner of William Street and Rudyerd Street and closed down as a public house in the 1970s. The building, which still exists, is now a shop.

ARK, 22 SAVILLE STREET
First recorded in 1822; last recorded in 1834.

ARTILLERY ARMS, 2 ALBION ROAD
First recorded in 1867; last recorded in the 1960s.
This pub stood on the corner of Albion Road and Norfolk Street.

BALLARAT, 42 SAVILLE STREET WEST AND 13 BOROUGH ROAD
First recorded in 1887; last recorded in 2007.
One of the more well-known hostelries in North Shields is the Ballarat Hotel, still occupying its original site on the south-east corner of Saville Street West and Borough Road. Often nicknamed 'The Rat', it derived its name from the town of Ballarat, in the state of Victoria, Australia, after the great rush to the Ballarat Goldfields during the mid-1800s. It is generally accepted that the origin of the name came from two aboriginal words, *Balla* and *Arat*, signifying a resting or camping place.

A busy Borough Road Corner, outside the Ballarat in 1927.

BALMORAL CASTLE, 4 STEPHENSON STREET
First recorded in: unknown; last recorded in: unknown.

BALMORAL HOUSE, CHURCH STREET
First recorded in 1895; last recorded in 1905.

BEDFORD ARMS (REFER TO: DUKE OF BEDFORD), 65 BEDFORD STREET

BEDFORD HOTEL (REFER TO: PHOENIX TAVERN AND FOUNTAIN HEAD),
91 BEDFORD STREET
First recorded in 1887; last recorded in 1887.

BELL AND BUCKET, NORFOLK STREET
First recorded in 1986; last recorded in 2007.
The fine stone building on the east side of Norfolk Street, which is now the Bell and Bucket, was originally the Union British School, which first opened in 1840. By 1906 it had been converted to accommodate North Shields' fire brigade, which remained here until 1959. The building was converted to a public house in 1986, with the unusual and catchy name being derived from its former use as a fire station.

BLUE BELL INN, BELLE VUE TERRACE
First recorded: unconfirmed; last recorded: pre-1822.
Prior to 1822, a Blue Bell Inn is recorded which is known to have stood in fields on the site of what is now the present Belle Vue Terrace, Coach Lane. No other information or details are known about this inn.

BLYTH AND TYNE HOTEL, 1 CHARLOTTE STREET, 1 LOWER PEARSON STREET
AND STEPHENSON STREET
First recorded in 1887; last recorded in 1940.
One of many corner site public houses in North Shields, the Blyth and Tyne Hotel was situated on
the north-east corner of Charlotte Street and Stephenson Street.

BOARD INN, 34 TYNE STREET
First recorded in 1847; last recorded in 1847.

BOILERMAKERS ARMS, 12 WELLINGTON STREET
First recorded in 1886; last recorded in 1886.
This pub was situated on the south-east corner of Wellington Street and Little Bedford Street.

BOROUGH ARMS, 29/61 CAMDEN STREET
First recorded in 1850; last recorded in 1910.
Also known as Ye Olde Boro' Arms, this was a small pub, situated on the west side of Camden Street.
After demolition, the site was occupied by part of the car park and access areas of the North Shields
Shopping Centre Mall to the rear of the present Central Library.

BOROUGH ARMS, 2 BOROUGH ROAD AND 26/28 GARDNER STREET
First recorded in 1865; last recorded in 1940.
The Borough Arms was situated on the north-east corner of Borough Road Bank and Gardner
Street. It was one of a small number of public houses in the area which retained the original glazed
terracotta faience and pub sign above the windows and entrance.

BREWERY ARMS, BEACON STREET
First recorded in 1850; last recorded in 1855.
Also known as the Brewers Arms and Brewery House, this building stood on the western side of
Beacon Street. It virtually backed on to the nearby Oak Tavern which stood on nearby Charlotte
Street.

BRIDGE INN (REFER TO: PUSH & PULL INN), 3 BEDFORD STREET

BRITANNIA VAULTS, 12 CHURCH STREET
First recorded in 1865; last recorded in 1920.
The Britannia Vaults, also known as the Britannia Inn, stood halfway between Charlotte Street and
Tyne Street, on the east side of Church Street, diagonally opposite the Kings Head.

BURTON HOUSE (REFER TO: SHAKESPEARE TAVERN), HOWARD STREET,
41 TYNE STREET AND NEWS ROOM BANK

CAMDEN ARMS, 12 CAMDEN STREET
First recorded in 1865; last recorded in 1865.

CASK & STILLAGE (REFER TO: WHITE HART), BEDFORD STREET

CENTRAL ARMS, 6 SAVILLE STREET WEST
First recorded in 1938; last recorded in 1938.

Tynemouth Road, looking east, *c.* 1908. The Langley Castle is the building with the bay window and roof sign of A.N. Dodds, and the Cobourg can be seen a short distance beyond.

CITY OF DUBLIN, 72 TYNE STREET
First recorded in 1887; last recorded in 1887.
Located on the bank side of Tyne Street, the City of Dublin stood almost opposite the foot of Norfolk Street.

CLOCK VAULTS, 4 TOLL STREET AND TOLL SQUARE.
First recorded in 1855; last recorded in 1930.
Originally known as the Clock Tavern, the Clock Vaults was situated on Toll Street, near to the corner with Toll Square.

CLOCK VAULTS, 30 BEDFORD STREET AND 33-34 WELLINGTON STREET
First recorded in 1887; last recorded in 1968.
The well-known Clock Vaults was one of the larger pubs in the High Town, and was an imposing building which stood on the south-east corner of Bedford Street and Wellington Street.

COBOURG HOTEL, 1 COBURG STREET AND 18/20/21 COBURG TERRACE
First recorded in 1887; last recorded in 2007.
Also known simply as the Coburg (originally and probably incorrectly spelled Cobourg), the building was situated on the corner of Coburg Terrace, (Tynemouth Road) and Coburg Street. Coburg Terrace is a sub-named street forming a short section of the north side of Tynemouth Road, between North King Street and Coburg Street. The name Coburg was probably derived from Queen Victoria's connection with Prince Albert, who was descended from the German House of Saxe-Coburg and Gotha. During the 1990s, the Coburg was renamed 'The Mash Tun' in an effort to renew its image: however, it proved to be an unpopular choice, and the pub reverted to its original name a short time afterwards.

The Colonel Linskill, Charlotte Street in 2006.

COLONEL LINSKILL, 17/34/35 CHARLOTTE STREET
First recorded in 1834; last recorded in 2007.
This pub took its name from William Linskill, who became the first mayor of Tynemouth in 1849. According to the Ordnance Survey Town Plan of 1896, the original Colonel Linskill Inn stood on the north side of Charlotte Street between King Street and Reed Street: however, over the years these streets were changed, lost to development, or renamed, so the original description of the location may be no longer applicable. The pub was demolished and rebuilt on the same site in 1937, and The Colonel Linskill is therefore now situated on Charlotte Street, on the corner of Kettlewell Terrace.

In 1986, the pub was renamed 'The Fog on the Tyne' in an effort to try and renew a somewhat tarnished image. The name was derived from a popular song title of the era, by the pop group 'Lindisfarne'. This change seemed to have little effect, and so it underwent a further name change in October 1992 to 'the Laurel Arms' in yet another attempt to rejuvenate the pub. This time, the name change was taken from Stan Laurel, of the famous Laurel and Hardy comedy duo, who was resident in nearby Dockwray Square during the early 1900s. Neither of these changes having had any effect, and the pub always being referred to as 'The Linskill', it reverted back to its original name a few years later.

COMMERCIAL HOTEL (& POSTING HOUSE), HOWARD STREET
First recorded in 1822; last recorded in 1865.
The Commercial Hotel was a large building situated on the east side of Howard Street, close to the end of Union Street.

CORPORATION ARMS, 9 WELLINGTON STREET
First recorded in 1855; last recorded in 1855.
The Corporation Arms stood on the western corner of Wellington Street and Church Way.
In 1834-1855 and 1857-1940, it was recorded as the Wellington House or Wellington Hotel.

CORPORATION ARMS, 125/126/127 LINSKILL STREET
First recorded in 1851; last recorded in 1940.

CORVETTE, CHARLOTTE STREET
First recorded in 1958; last recorded in the mid-1990s.
The Corvette stood at the eastern end of Charlotte Street, at the north-west corner of Beacon Street and Bird Street. It was built in 1958, on the site of the earlier Robin Hood pub. In latter years, the Corvette fell into decline, and it was demolished in the mid-1990s.

CRESCENT TAVERN, 83 HUDSON STREET
First recorded in 1822; last recorded in 1940.

CRITERION RESTAURANT, 11/12 TYNE STREET
First recorded in 1887; last recorded in 1940.
Also known simply as the Criterion, this pub was situated on the north side of Tyne Street, and stood between the junctions with Norfolk Street and Stephenson Street.

CROWN, BEACON STREET
First recorded in 1850; last recorded in 1850.

CROWN, 7/19 CAMDEN STREET
First recorded in 1855; last recorded in 1865.
The Crown was a small building which stood on the west side of Camden Street, a little to the south of its junction with Saville Street, on the area now occupied by a recently built supermarket.

CROWN & SCEPTRE, 29/184 STEPHENSON STREET
First recorded in 1850; last recorded in 1979.
Demolished in the late 1970s, the Crown & Sceptre stood on the west side of Stephenson Street, close to the junction with Saville Street. Until its demolition, the Crown & Sceptre was one of a small number of public houses in the area which retained the original glazed terracotta faience and pub signage above the windows and entrance.

CRYSTAL TAVERN. 43 HUDSON STREET
First recorded in 1867; last recorded in 1867.

CUSTOMS, 83 HUDSON STREET
First recorded in 1865; last recorded in 1865.

DUKE OF BEDFORD, 65/115 BEDFORD STREET
First recorded in 1850; last recorded in 1940.
The Duke of Bedford was situated on the west side of Bedford Street, just a few yards to the north of its junction with West Percy Street. The building, which still exists, was converted into a shop after its closure as a pub.

DUKE OF EDINBURGH, 9 UPPER PEARSON STREET AND 102 CHURCH STREET
First recorded in 1887; last recorded in 1940.
The Duke of Edinburgh was a large building which stood at the north-east corner of Upper Pearson Street and Church Street. This site is now occupied by part of North Shields police station.

DUKE OF SUSSEX, 43/45/80 CHURCH STREET
First recorded in 1850; last recorded in 1940.
This pub stood on the eastern corner of Church Street at its junction with Upper Pearson Street.

DUKE OF WELLINGTON, 55 CHURCH WAY
First recorded in 1850; last recorded in 1855.
Situated on the west side of Church Way, The Duke of Wellington was a small building, located a little to the north of its junction with Wellington Street, on which the name has a bearing.

DUKE OF YORK, 15 KING STREET
First recorded in 1822; last recorded in 1930.
Situated towards the bottom of, and on the eastern side of King Street, during the mid-1800s the Duke of York was one of the larger pubs of the High Town.

EAGLE INN, 9 UPPER PEARSON STREET
First recorded in 1855; last recorded in 1865.
The Eagle Inn stood in a prominent corner position at the south-east corner of Upper Pearson Street and Upper Church Street.

EARL GREY INN, 27/53 LINSKILL STREET, 14 LOWER PEARSON STREET AND 103/104 CHARLOTTE STREET
First recorded in 1834; last recorded in 1940.
The Earl Grey Inn was a corner building, situated on the east side of Linskill Street at the junction with Lower Pearson Street (later Charlotte Street). In common with other public houses of the same name in North Shields, the premises were probably named after Charles Grey, (2nd Earl Grey 1764–1845), a British politician who, as prime minister (1830–1834), implemented parliamentary and social reforms, notably the abolition of slavery throughout the British Empire.

EARL GREY, 15/16 HUDSON STREET
First recorded in 1850; last recorded in 1938.

EARL PERCY, STEPHENSON STREET
First recorded in 1822; last recorded in 1834.
This public house probably derived its name from Algernon George Percy, 6th Duke of Northumberland, KG (20 May 1810-2 January 1899), who was styled Earl Percy.

ELEPHANT AND CASTLE, 19 CAMDEN STREET
First recorded in 1850; last recorded in 1850.
An unusual combination of names for a pub, with two theories, the castle here being either the howdah on the back of an elephant, or possibly a corruption of Infanta de Castile, usually said to be a reference to Eleanor of Castile, the wife of Edward I (in Spain and Portugal, the infanta was the eldest daughter of the monarch without a claim to the throne).

EMPIRE, 72 TYNE STREET
First recorded in 1897; last recorded in 1912.

ESLINGTON HOUSE, 33 CAMDEN STREET
First recorded in 1834; last recorded in 1834.
The first known reference to Eslington is in 1334: it referred to a stone tower in the civil parish of Whittingham, Northumberland. It has not been established why this public house should bear a related name.

A view looking east along Railway Street, *c.* 1912. North Shields railway station is on the left, and the European and United States Hotel is visible to the immediate right of the picture.

EUROPEAN AND UNITED STATES, 5/11 RAILWAY TERRACE
First recorded in 1865; last recorded in 1968.
The unusually named European and United States (or County Hotel) as it was latterly known, stood opposite North Shields railway station, to the south side of Railway Terrace, between Rudyerd Street and Little Bedford Street.

EXPRESS INN, 6 NILE STREET
First recorded in 1938; last recorded in 1938.
Standing on the corner of Nile Street and Russell Street, the structure of this building still exists, and some time after closure as a public house, it became an amusement arcade.

FLINNS (REFER TO: NORTH EASTERN HOTEL), 42 NILE STREET AND 17 WEST PERCY STREET
First recorded in 1847; last recorded in 1897.
Originally referred to as the Spirit of Dublin Porter Vaults, these premises were renamed 'Flinns'. The building was demolished in order to make way for the North Eastern Hotel.

FLOWER POT, ALBION STREET AND 14 ALBION ROAD WEST
First recorded in 1822-1850 as The Flower Pot; last recorded in 1850-2007 as the Spring Gardens Inn.
The Flower Pot existed until 1850, when it was renamed the Spring Gardens Inn. It was a well-known landmark of its day, and was the first calling station in North Shields of the old stage coaches. The calling station for coaches is believed to have stood on this site since about 1690. The Flower Pot was renowned as an 'open-air' public house, as many of the tables were arranged in the large flower garden at the rear of the inn, which also had a large pond stocked with goldfish and was a great attraction in bygone days. The premises came into the possession of Newcastle Breweries, and in 1934, it was rebuilt to its present format, with the frontage being very similar in design to that of the Cannon at Billy Mill, and the Collingwood Arms at Chirton.

FOUNTAIN HEAD, 91 BEDFORD STREET
First recorded in 1897; last recorded in 1968.
Built on the site of the Old Phoenix Tavern, the Fountain Head stood on the west side of Bedford Street, slightly to the north of its junction with Wellington Street. Until its demolition in the 1970s to make way for new shops, the Fountain Head was one of a small number of public houses in the area which retained its original glazed terracotta faience and pub signage above the windows and entrance.

FREE GARDNERS ARMS, 57 CAMDEN STREET
First recorded in 1886; last recorded in 1905.

FRIENDLY TAVERN, CHURCH ROW AND 9/10 CHURCH WAY
First recorded in 1822; last recorded in 1865.

FUTURE ADMIRAL, WELLINGTON STREET
First recorded in 1847; last recorded in 1847.

GARDNERS ARMS, 50 RUDYERD STREET AND 1 GARDNER STREET
First recorded in 1938; last recorded in the late 1970s.
The Gardners Arms was named after Ralph Gardner, a brewer of Chirton Green, who petitioned Oliver Cromwell's Parliament in 1655 about the restrictions on trade placed by Newcastle. He wrote the petition from his prison cell and called it *England's Grievances Discovered*.

GARIBALDI ARMS, 37 CHURCH WAY
First recorded in 1865; last recorded in 1865.
Probably named after the Italian General and nationalist who led 1,000 volunteers in the capture of Sicily and Naples in 1860. This conquest led to the formation of the kingdom of Italy in 1861.

GARRICKS HEAD, 23/25/52 SAVILLE STREET
First recorded in 1822; last recorded in 2007.
Situated on the south side of Saville Street, the Garricks Head was so named as a tribute to David Garrick (1717-1779), a British actor and theatre manager who was considered the foremost Shakespearean player of his time. As one of North Shields' oldest public houses, it was originally a small building, with glazed brickwork and an adjacent covered alleyway: however, in recent years it was extended by alterations to the adjoining buildings, thereby enlarging the entire premises as far as the east corner of Camden Street.

The original part of the Garricks Head is one of a small number of public houses in the area which have retained their original glazed terracotta faiences as well as the pub signages above the windows and entrance. Although the pub dates prior to 1822, an ornamental glazed scroll above the door incorporates a date of 1899.

GENERAL HAVELOCK, 25/38/40/42 SAVILLE STREET AND 10 CAMDEN STREET
First recorded in 1865; last recorded in 1990s.
At one time, the General Havelock was one of the largest public houses in North Shields. The building dominated a corner site to the south side of Saville Street and the western side of Camden Street. It was named after Major General Sir Henry Havelock (1795-1857), a native of Bishopwearmouth, Sunderland, whose heroic successes during the Indian Mutiny of 1857 earned him considerable praise from military leaders, politicians and newspaper editors in Britain. He was hailed as an example of 'military excellence and devout character'. He became a popular hero, representing all that was

The famous George Tavern, King Street under demolition in the 1950s.

great about the British Empire in the mid-nineteenth century. While his popularity grew in Britain, Havelock was still fighting in India and probably never realised the extent of his fame.

Similarly, Sir Colin Campbell was in command of troops during the Indian Mutiny at this time, and the public house situated at the west end of Saville Street bears his name. The General Havelock pub was demolished in the late 1990s, and was replaced by a discount supermarket in 2007.

GEORGE TAVERN, 68/70/73 KING STREET
First recorded in 1800; last recorded in 1940.

The George Tavern was generally known as the 'Old George', and was situated on the western side, close to the foot of King Street near the junction with Charlotte Street. In 1800, when the streets of North Shields were badly maintained, and the neighbourhood above the bank top mostly consisted of fields, with only a few houses scattered here and there, there was one inn of which the folk of Shields were proud – the famous George Tavern in King Street.

This inn was of great importance in the history of North Shields, as it contained a large assembly room where the magistracy administered the law of the town. It was the centre of function and authority. The room was brilliantly lit by a large crystal chandelier, and the tea and other rooms were spacious and comfortable. Dance clubs held at the premises were exclusive, and members were carefully selected before being proposed or admitted, and only the most aristocratic residents of the town were allowed to join. The magnificent balls that were held there were very elaborate affairs: seated in the parlour, on ancient wheel-back armchairs, gigantic platefuls of English roast beef were partaken of, the firelight mellowing the old coaching prints that hung around the room.

The commemoration of the jubilee of King George, on 25 October 1809, was celebrated in the town by the ringing of Christ Church bells, and in the evening by a grand ball and supper in the George Tavern. The proceeds of this ball, augmented by general subscriptions, were devoted to the building of the Royal Jubilee School, for the education of poor girls and boys.

In the 1860s, Revd John Broadbent, a Wesleyan minister and temperance reformer, arrived in the town, and upon seeing the volume of drunkenness of the inhabitants, he worked with untiring energy until, under his Christian influence, a great change was effected in North Shields, to the betterment of the people both morally and spiritually. It was this single advocate of temperance who is said to have killed the popularity of the George Tavern.

GOLDEN FLEECE, 71/72 NORFOLK STREET
First recorded in 1865; last recorded in 1920.
Adjoining the side of St Columba's United Reformed church hall in Northumberland Square, the Golden Fleece was located on the west side of Norfolk Street. The building still exists to this day as a house, with an adjacent covered alleyway.

GOLDEN LION, CHURCH WAY
First recorded: not recorded; last recorded: not recorded.

GREENLAND FISHERY, CHARLOTTE STREET
First recorded in 1822; last recorded in 1834.
Presumably so named because of the local connection with the fishing trade.

GREYHOUND, BIRD STREET, BEACON STREET AND TOLL STREET
First recorded in 1822; last recorded in 1851.

GREYHOUND, 22/25 CHURCH STREET
First recorded in 1834; last recorded in 1855.

HOPE INN, 41 NORFOLK STREET
First recorded in 1855; last recorded in 1940.
The Hope Inn was situated on the east side of Norfolk Street, near to the old fire station (later converted to the Bell and Bucket pub).

HOWICK HALL, 9 BEDFORD STREET
First recorded in 1834; last recorded in 1834.
This public house was named after Howick Hall, the home of the Grey family from 1319. The best-known member of the family was the 2nd Earl Grey, who was the prime minister responsible for passing the Great Reform Bill of 1832, and whose monument stands at the top of Grey Street in Newcastle.

IMPERIAL ARMS, 19 CHURCH STREET
First recorded in 1887; last recorded in 1887.

JOHN BULL INN, 135 CHURCH STREET
First recorded in 1834; last recorded in 1920.
Also known as the John Bull Tavern, this was one of the smaller inns of the High Town, and stood on the west side of Church Street, not far from the junction with Lower Pearson Street (later to become Charlotte Street).

KING WILLIAM IV, 28 HUDSON STREET
First recorded in 1850; last recorded in 1855.
Named in honour of King William IV of Britain (1765-1837), this pub was located near the junction with Bird Street, and was a fairly insignificant building which stood on the west side of Hudson Street, backing onto James Square.

KINGS HEAD, 162/163 CHURCH STREET
First recorded in 1834; last recorded in 1912.
The Kings Head stood on the west side of Church Street, a short distance north of the junction with Tyne Street.

KINGS HEAD, 103 HUDSON STREET
First recorded in 1827; last recorded in 2007.
The Kings Head was originally a fairly small pub, standing on the high bank top, overlooking the Fish Quay from the foot of Hudson Street, near the junction with Tyne Street. Over the years, alteration work was carried out to extend the building to its present format, and during the 1990s it became another victim of change when, as an ailing pub, the name was changed to the Wooden Doll in an effort to increase its popularity. Over recent years it has supported live music, and tends to be a favourite venue for families, groups, and musicians.

LAMBTON CASTLE, 1-2 WELLINGTON STREET
First recorded in 1897; last recorded in 1981.
The Lambton Castle was a lock-up establishment with no residential accommodation, and stood on the north-east corner of Wellington Street at its junction with Little Bedford Street.

LANGLEY CASTLE, 16 COBOURG TERRACE AND 16 COBOURG STREET
First recorded in 1865; last recorded in 1930.
The Langley Castle stood on the north side of Tynemouth Road (Coburg Terrace) just a few yards west of the Coburg Hotel, and directly opposite the top of Hudson Street. The inn, which has since been converted to residential flats, is now numbered 102 and 104 Tynemouth Road.

LINSKILL ARMS, 1 GREY STREET
First recorded in 1865; last recorded in 1865.
The Linskill Arms was situated on the corner of Grey Street and North Church Street.

LORD BROUGHAM, CHURCH STREET
First recorded in 1834; last recorded in 1834.

LORD BYRON, 17/24 STEPHENSON STREET
First recorded in 1834; last recorded in 1920.
Named after Lord George Byron (1788-1824), the famous Anglo-Scottish poet, and situated diagonally opposite the Crown & Sceptre public house, the Lord Byron stood on the east side of Stephenson Street, not far from the junction with Saville Street/Charlotte Street.

LORD DELAVAL, 51 CHURCH STREET
First recorded in 1847; last recorded in 1847.

LORD HOWARTH, TOLL STREET
First recorded in 1834; last recorded in 1834.
No references can be found to ascertain why this public house was so named, or who Lord Howarth was, during the time this building existed.

LORD JOHN RUSSELL, 61 CAMDEN STREET
First recorded in 1834; last recorded in 1834.
This public house was named after John Russell, (1st Earl Russell, 1792–1878), a British politician who served as prime minister from 1846–1852 and 1865–1866, and advocated parliamentary reform.

LORD NELSON (REFER TO: ADMIRAL NELSON), 69 GEORGE STREET

Borough Road Corner, c. 1927, looking east along Saville Street. Three pubs are visible in this picture – the Mariners Arms, the Sir Colin Campbell Hotel and the Ballarat (to the immediate right).

LORD NELSON, TOLL STREET
First recorded in 1847; last recorded in 1852.

LORD NELSON, 31/32/63 CAMDEN STREET
First recorded in 1834; last recorded in 1968.
Named after Admiral Lord Horatio Nelson, the greatest hero in British naval history, this public house was a fairly small and innocuous building which stood on the east side of Camden Street near the junction with Saville Street. Eventually demolished, the site is now occupied by part of the multi-storey car park and service area of North Shields Shopping Mall.

MAGNESIA BANK, 1 CAMDEN STREET
First recorded in 1989; last recorded in 2007.
The Magnesia Bank is a relatively new public house. It opened in 1989, prior to which it had been better known as North Shields Central Club. Originally constructed as a commerce bank in the 1800s, and situated on the west side of Camden Street at the junction with Union Street, the building stood close to the steps leading from Union Street to the Low Town: known as Magnesia Bank Stairs, they loaned their name to the pub.

MARINERS ARMS, 1 SAVILLE STREET WEST
First recorded in 1938; last recorded in 2007.
Although the Mariners Arms was one of the older public houses in North Shields, the first directory listing did not appear until 1938. Situated opposite the Ballarat Hotel, it stands on the north-east

corner of Saville Street West and Borough Road. For many years, the Mariners Arms was simply an alehouse, as there was no licence to retail wines or spirits of any kind: however, an application was made in the 1970s to change this, and the appropriate spirit licence was subsequently granted.

In 1991, the name of the pub was changed to the 'Betty Baddoo', as a tribute to the previous landlady: however, this proved to be a very unpopular choice, and less than a year later, the name reverted back to its former and traditional name – the Mariners Arms.

MARINERS ARMS, CHURCH STREET
First recorded in 1850; last recorded in 1850.

MARQUIS OF GRANBY, 1 CHURCH STREET AND 31 TYNE STREET
First recorded in 1822; last recorded in 1940.
The Marquis of Granby was a corner inn, situated on the east side of Church Street at its junction with Tyne Street, and was always locally referred to simply as 'The Granby'. The Marquis of Granby was John Manners, a general in the eighteenth century who showed a great concern for the welfare of his men upon their retirement and provided funds for many to establish taverns – which were subsequently named after him.

MARQUIS OF LORNE, TYNEMOUTH ROAD, 15/16 PEARSON TERRACE AND UPPER QUEEN STREET
First recorded in 1887; last recorded in 1968.
The Marquis of Lorne formerly occupied a site on the south side of Tynemouth Road, at its junction on the west side of Upper Queen Street.

MASONS' ARMS, 64/161 STEPHENSON STREET
First recorded in 1850; last recorded in 1940.
The Masons' Arms stood on the west side of Stephenson Street, about halfway between Upper Pearson Street and Charlotte Street, on the site of what became the telephone exchange.

MASONIC ARMS, 70/71 BEDFORD STREET
First recorded in 1865; last recorded in 1928.
The Masonic, or Masons' Arms as it was sometimes known, was situated on the west side of Bedford Street, a few yards south of its junction with West Percy Street.

METERS ARMS, QUEEN STREET
First recorded in 1855; last recorded in 1855.
The unusually named Meters Arms was located on the east side of Queen Street, between Upper Pearson Street and Charlotte Street.

NAVIGATION TAVERN, 62 STEPHENSON STREET
First recorded in 1834; last recorded in 1834.

NEPTUNE TAVERN, TYNE STREET
First recorded in 1834; last recorded in 1834.

NEVILLE HOTEL, RAILWAY TERRACE AND 82 RUDYERD STREET
First recorded in 1865; last recorded in 2007.
The Neville Hotel stands on the west side of Rudyerd Street, at its junction with Railway Terrace.

NEWCASTLE INN, BEDFORD STREET
Situated on the west side of Bedford Street, opposite the Waterloo Tavern, the Newcastle Inn stood slightly to the south of the junction with West Percy Street.

NORFOLK ARMS, 77 NORFOLK STREET
First recorded in 1855; last recorded in 1855.
The Norfolk Arms was situated near to Northumberland Square, on the west side of Norfolk Street, beside the United Presbyterian church.

NORTH EASTERN HOTEL, 17/30 WEST PERCY STREET
First recorded in 1897; last recorded in 1968.
Built on the site of an earlier public house called 'Flinns', the North Eastern Hotel occupied a corner site on the north side of West Percy Road at the junction with Nile Street. The premises still exist and now accommodate a stationer's shop.

NORTHUMBERLAND ARMS, LITTLE BEDFORD STREET
First recorded in 1928; last recorded in 1940.
The Northumberland Arms was a small single-storey pub situated on the east side of Little Bedford Street, and was locally referred to as 'The Dead House'.

NORTHUMBERLAND HOTEL, 29/113 BEDFORD STREET AND LITTLE BEDFORD STREET
First recorded in 1822; last recorded in 1940.
The Northumberland Hotel was a single long building, situated between Bedford Street and Little Bedford Street, with entrances on both streets. It was located on the west side of Bedford Street, about halfway between the Tiger Stairs and Saville Street.

OAK TAVERN, 32 CHARLOTTE STREET
First recorded in 1850; last recorded in 1865.
The Oak Tavern was a small building situated on the south side of Charlotte Street, near to the junction with Beacon Street. It virtually backed on to the Brewers Arms which stood on nearby Beacon Street.

ODDFELLOWS ARMS, 56 GREY STREET
First recorded in 1938; last recorded in 1969.
This pub may have been named after its use as a meeting place by The Independent Order of Odd Fellows, a fraternal organisation derived from the English Oddfellows' Lodges of the mid-1700s.

ODDFELLOWS ARMS, ALBION ROAD
First recorded in 1980s; last recorded in 2007.
The present Oddfellows Arms on Albion Road was named after the original Oddfellows Arms which stood on Grey Street until around 1968. A relatively new pub, the present Oddfellows opened in the 1980s and occupies the building which, during the 1960s, was remembered by many people as the 'Karlson Club'.

OLD HIGHLANDER, 69 CHURCH WAY
First recorded in 1886; last recorded in 1887.

OLD INN, 51 NILE STREET
First recorded in 1865; last recorded in 1865.

OLD POST OFFICE INN, 20/65 TYNE STREET AND POST OFFICE STAIRS
First recorded in 1850; last recorded in 1899.
The Old Post Office Inn was set slightly back from the road on the bank side of Tyne Street, where it accommodated the long set of ninety-seven steps known as the Post Office Stairs which dropped down to Bell Street in the Low Town.

PERCY ARMS, 24/38/50 WEST PERCY STREET
First recorded in 1855; last recorded in 1930.
The Percy Arms was situated on the north side of West Percy Street between Nelson Street and Sidney Street.

PERSIMMON ARMS, 4 NILE STREET
First recorded in 1869; last recorded in 1932.

PHOENIX TAVERN, 55/68/70/91/111 BEDFORD STREET
First recorded in 1822 as the Phoenix Tavern; last recorded in 1887 as the Bedford Hotel.
The Phoenix Tavern was also known by a variety of names, including the Old Phoenix Tavern, the Phoenix Hotel and the New Phoenix. Situated on the west side of Bedford Street, it stood a little to the north of its junction with Wellington Street, and in 1887 was better known as the Bedford Hotel. After it was demolished, the 'Fountain Head' was built on the same site.

PINEAPPLE, 52/53/153 KING STREET, UPPER PEARSON STREET AND GEORGE STREET
First recorded in 1855; last recorded in 1940.
The Pineapple was a corner pub, prominently situated on the north-east corner of King Street and Upper Pearson Street.

POST BOY, 42 STEPHENSON STREET
First recorded in 1850; last recorded in 1865.
The Post Boy stood on the east side of Stephenson Street, and slightly to the north of its junction with Charlotte Street.

PRINCE ALBERT, 39 CHURCH STREET
First recorded in 1869; last recorded in 1871.

PRIORY INN, 2 ALBERT TERRACE
First recorded in: not recorded; last recorded in: not recorded.

PUSH AND PULL INN, 3 BEDFORD STREET
First recorded in 1850 as the Push and Pull Inn; last recorded in 1899 as the Bridge Inn.
The Push and Pull Inn was situated almost at the foot of, and on the east side of, Bedford Street. It occupied a situation on the steepest part of the road, backing onto Church Stairs. By 1887, it had been renamed the Bridge Inn, probably named after the nearby area called Wooden Bridge.

The Queens Head, Albion Road in 2006.

QUEENS HEAD, TURNPIKE ROAD, 8/11 ALBION STREET AND 13/14 ALBION ROAD
First recorded in 1822; last recorded in 2007.

When Queen Victoria ascended the throne in 1837, her name became quite the rage and was applied to all manner of things. This house, which stands on the south-east corner of Church Way and Albion Road, was originally called 'The Kings Head' before the then landlord, William Weatherilt, changed the name to 'the Victoria Inn', and accompanied the name change by fixing a painted portrait of the 'maiden monarch' as the signboard of his inn. In later years, the name of the inn changed from 'the Victoria Inn' to 'the Queens Head'.

For many years afterwards, the inn was affectionately known as 'the Church House' because of its close relationship with Christ Church, which stood opposite. On christening days, it is said that men stood around in readiness to take upon themselves the responsibilities of godfathers for a shilling, returning to the inn to drink the fee! On marriage occasions, a bride, when otherwise unprovided for, could be 'given away' on the same easy terms as those required for christenings. Women, after being 'churched', sometimes required a stimulant for nervous exhaustion. After burials in the church yard, a 'sit-down' by the underbearers became a regular thing. Bell-ringing also contributed its quota to the good of the house, for the bell-ringers in those days sometimes drank at the inn from the finish of the Sunday morning peal until their bell-tower ascent in the afternoon.

The stagecoaches running between Shields and Newcastle, and between Shields and Blyth, took up and set off passengers here. Coachmen would chat with the landlord or landlady, and there were generally two or three servant girls to assist with the luggage. In recent years the premises have been extended into the ajoining shop, situated on Church Way.

QUEENS HEAD, LOWER PEARSON STREET
First recorded in: not recorded; last recorded in: not recorded.

The Queens Head stood on the north side of Lower Pearson Street (later Charlotte Street), at its junction with Queen Street.

RABY CASTLE, 38 TYNE STREET
First recorded in 1834; last recorded in 1834.

RAILWAY TAVERN (REFER TO: UNCLE TOM'S CABIN), 51 BEDFORD STREET

RAILWAY HOTEL, 6 RAILWAY STREET AND LITTLE BEDFORD STREET
First recorded in 1850-1885 as the Railway Hotel; in 1886-1887 as the Rutherford Hotel; last recorded in 1897-1930 as the Station Hotel.
This building was situated on the south side of Railway Street at the north corner with Little Bedford Street. It underwent three name changes during its lifetime.

RAILWAY INN, 63 NILE STREET
First recorded in 1865; last recorded in the 1990s.
As the name suggests, the building took its name from North Shields railway station which, separated by an alleyway on the west side of Nile Street, stood directly next to it. In 1861, the building was known as the Railway Inn, later to become the Railway Hotel, (not be confused with another premises by the name of the Railway Hotel which stood directly opposite on the east side of the road). The building was one of a handful in the town which had a glazed terracotta faience, and ornamental signage above the windows and doors; however, after it closed down as a public house during the 1990s, the premises were converted to accommodate an amusement arcade. The original brown glazed terracotta faience is still apparent, but modern plastic signage covers the original ornamental pub name.

RED LION INN, CHURCH ROAD, 37/103/104/105 CHURCH WAY AND 27
WELLINGTON STREET
First recorded in 1757; last recorded in 1940.
It is very difficult to imagine that the Red Lion Inn, also known as the Old Red Lion, was at one time a popular roadside inn, which stood in the midst of green fields and hawthorn hedges, at a time when Church Way was nothing more than a narrow road, lined on each side by green hedgerows, and not another house within call. It was probably one of the oldest inns recorded in North Shields, and is shown on a plan of the Manor of Tynemouth dated 1757. The pub was demolished by the then owner, Mr A.N. Dodds, who later rebuilt the premises on the corner of Church Way and Wellington Street, backing on to Camden Lane.

REGATTA TAVERN, 49 TYNE STREET
First recorded in 1850 as the Regatta Tavern; last recorded in 1912 as the Turf Hotel.
The Regatta Tavern was a small pub which stood at the top of the bank side on the south side of Tyne Street, almost opposite the junction with Linskill Street. It was renamed the Turf Hotel some time prior to 1897.

RISING SUN INN, 1 BEACON STREET AND TYNE STREET
First recorded in 1850; last recorded in 1940.
The Rising Sun Inn was a corner pub, situated on the bank top, at the south-west corner of Beacon Street and Tyne Street, opposite the original High Beacon Lighthouse and forming part of Trinity Buildings.

RISING SUN, 4 TOLL STREET
First recorded in 1834; last recorded in 1834.
Although recorded as a separate public house, because of its close proximity, it is likely that this is the same building as the Rising Sun Inn, situated on the corner of Beacon Street and Tyne Street.

ROBIN HOOD, 21 BEACON STREET AND BIRD STREET
First recorded in 1850; last recorded in 1957.
The Robin Hood was situated at the eastern end of Charlotte Street, at the north-west corner of Beacon Street and Bird Street. The building suffered a small amount of bomb damage in 1941, and was demolished in 1957, to be replaced by 'the Corvette' pub.

ROCKCLIFF ARMS, 15 BEDFORD STREET
First recorded in 1897; last recorded in 1897.

ROSE AND CROWN, TYNE STREET
First recorded in 1855; last recorded in 1855.
High on the bank top and adjoining Turpin's Bank Stairs, the Rose and Crown stood opposite the foot of Stephenson Street, at its junction with Tyne Street.

ROYAL ARMS, 49/59/60-61 NILE STREET
First recorded in 1850; last recorded in 2007.
The Royal Arms is a Victorian building, situated on the west side of Nile Street, at its junction with Russell Street. The pub bears the unofficial nickname 'Charlie Robsons', which was derived from a well-respected manager called Charles Robson, who ran the pub during the war years from 1936 and well into the 1940s. Despite many changes of management since then, and up to the present day, the pub is still locally referred to as 'Charlie's', or 'Charlie Robson's'.

RUTHERFORD HOTEL (REFER TO: RAILWAY HOTEL), 6 RAILWAY STREET

SADDLE INN, 5/7 NORFOLK STREET
First recorded in 1850; last recorded in 1899.
The Saddle Inn was situated on the east side of Norfolk Street, not far from the junction with Tyne Street.

SAW MILL INN, NORTHUMBERLAND STREET
First recorded in 1852; last recorded in 1852.

SHADES, RANTERS BANK AND HOWARD STREET
First recorded in 1850; last recorded in 1865.
This unusually named pub occupied the lower floor of the Old Subscription Library and Maritime Chambers, which later became the Stag Line offices.

SHAKESPEARE TAVERN, HOWARD STREET, 41 TYNE STREET AND NEWS ROOM BANK
First recorded in 1855 as the Shakespeare Tavern; last recorded in 1938 as Burton House.
The Shakespeare Tavern shared its name with another inn of the same name on nearby Clive Street, in the Low Town. The building was located on the bank side, at the foot of Howard Street, behind buildings on the south side of Tyne Street with News Room Stairs running alongside and down the bank to Liddell Street. The name was changed in later years to the Burton House, which may have been to avoid confusion with the Shakespeare Inn on nearby Clive Street.

SHIP, TOLL SQUARE
First recorded in 1822; last recorded in 1827.

A sketch of Spring Gardens Inn when it was built in 1934. Externally, it has hardly changed to this day.

SHIPWRIGHTS ARMS, CHURCH WAY
First recorded in 1855; last recorded in 1855.
The Shipwrights Arms stood on the west side of Church Way, a little to the south of its junction with Saville Street.

SHOULDER OF MUTTON, 19 WELLINGTON STREET
First recorded in 1822; last recorded in 1834.

SIR COLIN CAMPBELL, 3 SAVILLE STREET WEST
First recorded in 1865; last recorded in 2007.
The Sir Colin Campbell public house is situated on the north side of Saville Street West, diagonally opposite the Ballarat Hotel. During its lifetime, the front of the building was completely altered, almost being rebuilt. The pub was named as a tribute to Field Marshall Sir Colin Campbell (also known as Lord Clyde), who was an outstanding soldier. Born in Glasgow in 1792, Campbell fought in the Peninsular Wars (1808-14), the Sikh War (1848-49), the Crimean War (1854), and the Indian Mutiny of 1857. Campbell died in 1863, and is buried in Westminster Abbey (London). He is remembered for his personal bravery and, as a senior commander, for the cautious and considered prosecution of his various campaigns which saved the lives of many of his men.

SPIRIT OF DUBLIN PORTER VAULTS (REFER TO: FLINNS), NILE STREET AND WEST PERCY STREET
Originally called the Spirit of Dublin Porter Vaults, and standing on the corner of Nile Street and West Percy Street, these premises later became better known as Flinns.

SPRING GARDENS INN (REFER TO: FLOWER POT), ALBION STREET AND 14 ALBION ROAD WEST

STANLEY ARMS, 70 RUDYERD STREET AND 1–2 STANLEY STREET
First recorded in 1865; last recorded in 2007.
The Stanley Arms was named after the SS *Stanley*, which ran aground on the Black Middens in 1864. The pub, which occupies a corner site at the junction of Stanley Street and Rudyerd Street, has an original stained-glass fanlight window depicting the steamship, probably the only original item left on the premises which has seen several modernisations over its lifespan. The pub is still operating to this day.

STAR, 19 CAMDEN STREET
First recorded in 1834; last recorded in 1834.

STAR, 1/2/4 WELLINGTON STREET
First recorded in 1850; last recorded in 1887.
The Star Inn was a small building occupying a site on the north side of Wellington Street, near the junction with Little Bedford Street.

STATION HOTEL (REFER TO RAILWAY HOTEL), 6 RAILWAY STREET

SUN, STEPHENSON STREET
First recorded in 1822; last recorded in 1827.

TEAC FIDDLERS (REFER TO: ALNWICK CASTLE), SAVILLE STREET

TELEGRAPH HOTEL, 3 NILE STREET
First recorded in 1865; last recorded in 1968.
The Telegraph Hotel was located on the east side of Nile Street, directly opposite North Shields railway station. Ordnance Survey maps from 1861 indicate that it was originally called the Railway Hotel, but by 1896 it had been renamed The Telegraph Hotel, probably to avoid confusion with the similarly named and larger Railway Inn (Hotel) which stood on the opposite side of the road. The building, which still exists since its closure as a public house, has been converted into a shop.

TERRACE INN, 1 EAST STEPHENSON STREET, 1 DALE TERRACE AND
TYNEMOUTH ROAD
First recorded in 1855; last recorded in 1940.
The Terrace Inn stood almost directly opposite the Brandling Terrace Memorial church: the inn actually stood on the corner of East Stephenson Street at its junction with Tynemouth Road. (East Stephenson Street has long since been demolished and redeveloped, and is now occupied by the Magistrate's Court and part of the police station).

THREE BULL'S HEADS, 2 ALBION ROAD
First recorded in 1938; last recorded in 1938.

TIGER INN, 123 BEDFORD STREET
First recorded in 1855; last recorded in 1928.
A well-known landmark, the Tiger Stairs are one of the most famous sets of bank stairs in North Shields, and the Tiger Inn occupied a position immediately next to and on the south side of these steps. Whether the Tiger Inn was named after the stairs, or whether the Tiger Stairs were named after the inn is open to debate!

A derelict Tiger Inn, Bedford Street, in the 1930s.

TURF HOTEL (REFER TO: REGATTA TAVERN), 49 TYNE STREET AND CHURCH ROW

TURF HOTEL, CHURCH ROW
First recorded in 1827; last recorded in 1827.
A directory listing dated 1827 exists for the Turf Hotel, Church Row, however, there is evidence from other directories that the name 'the Turf Hotel' only came into being sometime between 1850 and 1897, when the Regatta Tavern on Church Row changed its name. Although unusual, it is possible that there were two premises in close proximity going by the same name.

TURKS HEAD, 6/10 LINSKILL STREET
First recorded in 1850; last recorded in 1938.
The Turks Head stood on the east side of Linskill Street, just a few yards north of the junction with Tyne Street.

TURNPIKE GATE, LINSKILL STREET
First recorded in 1834; last recorded in 1834.
A turnpike is a road paid for partly or wholly by fees collected from travellers at toll gates. It derives its name from the hinged bar that prevented passage through such a gate until the payment of the toll. The pub possibly derived its name from one of the nearby turnpike roads.

TYNE INN, 42/43 CAMDEN STREET
First recorded in 1822; last recorded in 1850.
This inn was situated on Camden Street at the corner with Wellington Street. This area is now enclosed by the North Shields Shopping Mall.

Uncle Tom's Cabin, *c.* 1895.

TYNEMOUTH CASTLE TAVERN, 19/42 CHURCH STREET
First recorded in 1850; last recorded in 1865.
The Tynemouth Castle Tavern was situated on the east side of Church Street, just a little to the south of the junction with Lower Pearson Street (Charlotte Street).

UNCLE TOM'S CABIN, 25/26/51 BEDFORD STREET
First recorded in 1850-1855 as the Railway Tavern; last recorded in 1855-1968 as Uncle Tom's Cabin.
Uncle Tom's Cabin, also known as Uncle Tom's Vaults, was certainly one of the most famous public houses that ever existed in North Shields. Originally called the Railway Tavern, it was renamed Uncle Tom's Cabin in around 1855 after the success of the 1852 novel by the same name, written by Harriet Beecher Stowe.

   During much of the pub's latter-day life, it was perhaps most notoriously remembered for the many brawls and fights which occurred there, and was affectionately nicknamed 'The Flying Stool'. The building stood on the east side of Bedford Street, not far from the junction with Saville Street, and was demolished during the late 1960s and '70s development phase, to be eventually replaced by part of the North Shields Shopping Mall.

VICTORIA HOTEL, 1 ALBERT TERRACE AND TYNEMOUTH ROAD
First recorded in 1938; last recorded in 2007 as The Tap & Spile.
Another victim of the time when it was fashionable to change the name of a long-established public house, the Victoria, on Tynemouth Road, was altered in 1989 to 'The Tap & Spile'. This name has remained with the premises to the present day.

A 1950s view of the Victoria Inn, William Street.

VICTORIA HOTEL (REFER TO:YE OLDE HUNDRED), ALBION ROAD
First recorded in 1855-1897 as the Victoria Hotel; last recorded in 1897-2007 as Ye Olde Hundred.

Originally called the Victoria Inn, this building was situated next door to the Angel Hotel on the south-west corner of Albion Road and Church Way. Just prior to 1897, the Victoria and the Angel were converted to form a single larger building, which became better known as Ye Olde Hundred.

Early directories list the addresses as 69 Church Way and sometimes as 15 Albion Road: however, after many of the properties were renumbered during the late 1800s, the address of the pub became 100 Church Way, from which the name of the pub is derived.

VICTORIA INN, BOROUGH ROAD AND 19 WILLIAM STREET
First recorded in 1865; last recorded in 2007.

Also known as the Victoria Hotel, and occupying a corner site at the western end of William Street at its junction with Borough Road, the Victoria is one of the few old North Shields pubs still standing to this day.

VOLUNTEER ARMS, 37 CHURCH WAY
First recorded in 1887; last recorded in 1930.

Also recorded as the Red Lion Inn, the Volunteer Arms stood on the west side of Church Way, a little to the north of its junction with Wellington Street. The site is now occupied by part of the North Shields Shopping Mall.

WATERLOO INN, 54/103/109 BEDFORD STREET
First recorded in 1834; last recorded in 1865.
Situated on the east side of Bedford Street, opposite the Newcastle Inn, the Waterloo Inn, or Waterloo Tavern as it was sometimes known, stood slightly to the south of the junction with West Percy Street.

WELLINGTON HOTEL, CHURCH WAY AND 5/8/9 WELLINGTON STREET
First recorded in 1834; last recorded in 1940.
Also recorded as the Corporation Arms in 1855, the Wellington Hotel, or Wellington House, stood on the north-west corner of Wellington Street and Church Way.

WHITE HART, 49 BEDFORD STREET/95 BEDFORD STREET
First recorded in 1850; last recorded in 2001.
The White Hart occupied a site on the east side of Bedford Street, midway between the junctions with West Percy Street and Wellington Street. A narrow lane next to the pub connected Bedford Street with Church Way.

The white hart ('hart' is an old word for stag) was the personal badge of Richard II, who derived it from the arms of his mother, Joan, 'The Fair Maid of Kent', heiress of Edmund of Woodstock. The National Gallery, London has a portrait of Richard II wearing a gold and enamelled white hart jewel. Pictures of the angels surrounding the Virgin Mary are often depicted wearing white hart badges, and in English folklore, the white hart is associated with Herne the Hunter. There are still many inns and pubs in England that show the sign of the white hart.

By 1993, the pub had developed a somewhat tarnished image, and in an effort to overcome this, it was renamed as the Cask & Stillage. The name change, however, was short-lived and in 2001 the pub closed its doors for the last time. Although the building still exists, it was subsequently converted into two shops.

WHITE SWAN, UPPER PEARSON STREET
First recorded in: unconfirmed; last recorded in: unconfirmed.
The White Swan was a small inn, which stood on the south side of Upper Pearson Street, close to the corner of Linskill Street, and directly opposite to where the present police station now stands.

WILLIAM IV, 28 HUDSON STREET
First recorded in: unconfirmed; last recorded in: unconfirmed.

WILLIAM IV, 29 STEPHENSON STREET
First recorded in 1834; last recorded in 1834.

WINDSOR CASTLE, LINSKILL STREET
First recorded in 1834; last recorded in 1834.

WOODEN BRIDGE HOUSE, BEDFORD STREET
First recorded in 1865; last recorded in 1865.
Although unconfirmed, this may actually be the same pub as the Bridge Inn (Push and Pull), situated at 3 Bedford Street.

WOODEN DOLL (REFER TO: KINGS HEAD), 103 HUDSON STREET

YE OLD HUNDRED (REFER TO: ANGEL HOTEL & VICTORIA HOTEL), 15 ALBION ROAD, 69 CHURCH WAY AND 100 ALBION ROAD

Chapter Three

North Shields Bull Ring Area

ABERLLOLWYN ARMS, SOUTH STREET AND 27 FRONT STREET
First recorded in 1865; last recorded in 1932.
In 1895, Aberllolwyn Hall was recorded as a private residence within Llan-y-chaiarn, a small parish and village in the county of Cardigan, two miles south of Aberystwyth. There appear to be very few references to Aberllolwyn, and as there is no apparent significance to the distinctly Welsh title given to the pub, the reason for its name remains a mystery. The pub was situated on the south-eastern corner of South Street (Dock Road) and closed in 1932. It was later demolished.

ANCHOR TAVERN, 14/18 DUKE STREET AND SWANS QUAY
First recorded in 1834; last recorded in 1865.

BAY HORSE, 39 DUKE STREET AND FERRYBOAT LANDING
First recorded in 1834; last recorded in 1855.
Situated next to the riverside near to the Ferry Landing on Duke Street, the Bay Horse was accessed via an alleyway situated between the Steam Ferry House and the Sussex Arms.

BEE HIVE INN, 12/31 DOTWICK STREET
First recorded in 1822; last recorded in 1899.
Smaller than the neighbouring Clarendon Hotel, the Bee Hive Inn was situated a little further south on the west side of Dotwick Street. It has long since been demolished.

BERWICK ARMS, 1 TRINITY STREET, 2 TRINITY TERRACE AND 2 COACH LANE
First recorded in 1887; last recorded in 2007.
The Berwick Arms is situated on the north corner of Coach Lane and Trinity Street. Externally, this is probably the most decorative public house in North Shields, as the external façade construction consists of ornate glazed coloured brickwork and terracotta tiles. It was one of a small number of public houses in North Shields faced in this style.

BLACK BULL, BULL RING AND COLLINGWOOD STREET
First recorded in 1822; last recorded in 1827.

BLUE BELL, BULL RING AND COLLINGWOOD STREET
First recorded in: not recorded; last recorded in: not recorded.

BOARD, NEW QUAY
First recorded in 1834; last recorded in 1834.

BREWERY INN, 2 BULL RING
First recorded in 1887; last recorded in 1899.
The Brewery Inn stood on the east side of the Bull Ring between the Bull Ring Inn and the Essex Arms.

BULL RING INN, 3/10 BULL RING
First recorded in 1822; last recorded in 1930.
The Bull Ring Inn, (and later, the New Bull Ring), stood in the south-west corner of the Bull Ring, close to the Dock Inn, and separated by Grey Horse Quay. There have been three pubs of this name built on the same site, all of which have long since disappeared.

BURDON MAIN, DUKE STREET AND DOTWICK STREET
First recorded in 1822; last recorded in 1865.
The Burdon Main or Burdon Arms is recorded in directories as being situated on both Duke Street and Dotwick Street. These streets were only a short distance apart in the Bull Ring area of North Shields.

CANNON INN, 14 NORTH STREET AND MILBURN PLACE
First recorded in 1893; last recorded in 1906.
Now demolished.

CENTURIAN ARMS, BULL RING AND COLLINGWOOD STREET
First recorded in 1834; last recorded in 1865.
The Centurian was a large building on the Bull Ring, dominating a corner site at the north end of Dotwick Street. To the rear, the building adjoined The Dock House, at the corner of Dotwick Street and Dock Lane.

CHAIN LOCKER (REFER TO CRANE HOUSE), 44/50 DUKE STREET

Opposite: The Bull Ring, near Duke Street, North Shields in 1912.

Right: A map of North Shields Low Town, showing some of the prominent streets, banks, stairs and quays between the Bull Ring and Clifford's Fort.

CLARENDON HOTEL, 35/36 DOTWICK STREET
First recorded in 1887; last recorded in 1899.

The Clarendon Hotel was a large building which stood to the west side of Dotwick Street, opposite the head of one of the huge Graving Docks. An Ordnance Survey map dated 1857 indicates that the hotel occupied the site of two earlier public houses – The Hylton Castle and the Vulcan's Arms. The pub was probably named after George William Frederick Villiers, 4th Earl of Clarendon, (1800–1870), a British statesman who was ambassador to Spain during the Carlist War and then Lord Privy seal. As Lord Lieutenant of Ireland, he made efforts to ease disorder and distress during the famine and was foreign secretary (1853–58) during the Crimean War.

COACH AND HORSES, DUKE STREET AND 20 BULL RING
First recorded in 1822; last recorded in 1834.

COAL WAGGON, CHORLTON PLACE
First recorded in 1827; last recorded in 1827.

COLLINGWOOD MAIN, NORTH STREET
First recorded in 1827; last recorded in 1827.

CORNER HOUSE, BULL RING
First recorded in 1827; last recorded in 1827.

CRANE HOUSE, 44/50 DUKE STREET
First recorded in 1834; last recorded in 2004.

Situated on the west side of Duke Street, near to the present ferry landing stage, the Crane House was a corner building believed to have been named after a dockside crane, a picture of which was incorporated within the original glasswork of the premises.

The Crane House has stood on this site since at least 1850: however, it was rebuilt in 1905 from a design by Joseph Oswald and Son, and renamed as the Crane House Vaults. Previously owned by

More commonly known as the Crane House, or Crane House Vaults, this picture of the Crane Hotel dates to around 1910.

W.H. Allison & Co., Wine & Spirit Merchants and Brewers, of North Shields, the premises came into the possession of Newcastle Breweries on its formation in 1890. The new building was styled in brown glazed brickwork on the lower level, and was one of a small number of public houses in the area which retained the original glazed terracotta faience. Internally, there was a front bar with a rear sitting room, served by a single bar counter, with a hatch to the rear room.

In the early 1900s, the Crane House was the last building in Duke Street, a narrow street which led to the rear of the docks to the south via the Bull Ring. By the end of the First World War, most of the buildings on the south side of Duke Street had been demolished, but the Crane House managed to survive, standing alone at the end of the New Quay. Latterly, the pub underwent a name change on a nautical theme to be known as 'the Chain Locker', but in 2004 it closed its doors as a public house for the last time, and with its remaining listed frontage, it was incorporated into a new housing development where its heritage is preserved.

CROWN AND THISTLE, 41 DUKE STREET
First recorded in 1822; last recorded in 1855.
The Crown and Thistle stood on the west side of Duke Street, adjacent to Kirby's Bank Stairs, and adjoined the Crane House Vaults.

DOCK HOTEL, NORTHUMBERLAND DOCK
First recorded c. 1870; last recorded in 1974.
The Dock Hotel, or Dock House, was located near Northumberland Dock, and has existed since the 1870s. The house was run by members of the Beck family since that time, and locally, the pub has always been known as 'Minnie Beck's'. The original licensee was a William Gibson, followed in the 1920s by his daughter, Jane Beck, and subsequently in 1942 by her daughter, Mary Ann Beck, (affectionately and locally known as Minnie Beck). Minnie Beck ran the pub in the name of her brother, George. Throughout its lifespan, the Dock Hotel had no licence to sell wines or spirits and was purely a typical old alehouse: however, Minnie bent the rules by serving spirits from under the counter, and managed to evade prosecution during her term as landlady by simply being a firm judge of who had had enough to drink.

Minnie Beck was a teetotaller who would refuse to serve anyone she did not know, or whom she did not like, and rather than allow rowdiness, she would simply close the house. Aged eighty-six in July 1973, the pub closed after Minnie Beck was attacked and savagely beaten in her bedroom

Famously known as 'Minnie Beck's', this picture of the Dock Hotel was taken in the 1930s.

following a burglary. The Dock Hotel was demolished in 1974, during the time that Minnie was hospitalised, but she never fully recovered, and died in 1976.

DOCK HOUSE, DOTWICK STREET
First recorded in 1850; last recorded in 1855.
The Dock House was a large building which stood on the corner of Dotwick Street and Dock Lane, and adjoined the Centurian public house to the north.

DOCK INN, 60 NORTH STREET
First recorded in 1855; last recorded in 1940.
The Dock Inn, later to become the New Dock Inn, was situated on the north-west corner of North Street, at its junction with East Street, in the area referred to as Mount Pleasant. It is likely that it derived its name from the opening of the nearby Smith's Docks in 1852.

DOCK INN, 7 BULL RING
First recorded in 1822; last recorded in 1865.
The Dock Inn stood in the south-west corner of the Bull Ring, close to the Bull Ring Inn, and separated by Grey Horse Quay.

DUKE OF PORTLAND, COLLINGWOOD STREET (EXACT LOCATION UNCONFIRMED)
First recorded in 1834; last recorded in 1834.
The Duke of Portland is a peerage title created in 1716 for Henry Bentinck, who was already Earl of Portland. The Dukedom of Portland became extinct on the 9th Duke's death in 1990, though the 9th Duke's distant cousin succeeded him as Earl of Portland. The ducal seat was Welbeck Abbey, Nottinghamshire. There is no obvious reason as to why a public house in North Shields was given this name.

ESSEX ARMS, 2/23 DUKE STREET
First recorded in 1850; last recorded in 1887.
The Essex Arms was situated at the south end of Duke Street, at the edge of the Bull Ring.

Above left: The Dock Inn, North Street, *c.* 1930.

Above right: Golden Fleece, Duke Street, *c.* 1925.

FALCON ARMS, 37 DOTWICK STREET
First recorded in 1865; last recorded in 1865.
The pub name is likely to have been derived from the ancient sport of falconry.

FERRY HOUSE, 1 DUKE STREET AND NEW QUAY
First recorded in 1822; last recorded in 1887.
There have been several derivations of the name of this public house, which was generally and simply known as 'The Ferry'. It was one of the smallest public houses in North Shields. Originally called the Steam Ferry House or Steam Packet, and sometimes referred to as the Steamboat, it was shortened to the Ferry House, and was a small inn, which took its name from the Steam Ferry Station which stood only a few yards away on the river. Situated on the east side of Duke Street, directly opposite the Crane House Vaults and the Crown and Thistle, it was separated by a narrow alleyway from the Sussex Arms. The inn stood next to Grindstone Stairs, an alleyway which ran from Duke Street and ended with a set of steps to the riverside.

GOLDEN FLEECE, 11 NEW QUAY
First recorded in 1834-1984 as the Golden Fleece; last recorded in 2007 as the Porthole.
Situated to the east side of Clive Street, at the foot of Borough Road (Bank) junction, the Golden Fleece is the most southerly of all the inns and taverns on Clive Street, with the front of the building facing Duke Street and the New Quay. A Golden Fleece has stood on this site since the mid-1800s, and the present structure, rebuilt in 1897, stood just a few feet away from the Old Black Lion and the Percy Arms, to the rear of Steam Mill Lane and Clive Street.

The first Golden Fleece was only half the size of the present structure, and was approximately sixty years old when it was demolished to make way for the existing building, which was designed by W. & T.R. Milburn of Sunderland. The unusual architecture consists of a central first-floor arched balcony, which is dominated on each side by two ornate gables, each of which are topped with a sandstone finial. A decorative oriel multi-paned window and a semi-circular arched multi-paned window adorn the ground floor of the premises, which has remained unchanged since it was built.

Originally, the pub had a long single counter which served an 'L' shaped bar and five small sitting rooms. Modernisation over recent years has meant that much of the original interior splendour has been lost with lowered ceilings, rooms opened out and a background theme based on the interior of a ship, hence the change of name in the mid 1980s to 'The Porthole'.

At the end of the nineteenth century, there were more than 100 public houses along the length of North Shields' riverside, and this is one of the last remaining. In 2004, the building was considered to be of special architectural or historic interest, and was granted Grade II listed building status.

GREY HORSE, BULL RING
First recorded in 1822; last recorded in 1834.

HARE AND HOUNDS, COLLINGWOOD STREET
First recorded in 1847; last recorded in 1847.

HOPE AND ANCHOR, DUKE STREET (EXACT LOCATION UNCONFIRMED)
First recorded in 1822; last recorded in 1827.
A common name for many public houses throughout the country, the name takes its origin from the Bible – Hebrews 6:19: 'We have this as a sure and steadfast anchor of the soul, a hope'.

HYLTON CASTLE, 28 DOTWICK STREET
First recorded in 1850; last recorded in 1855.
The Hylton Castle stood directly next door to the Vulcan's Arms Castle public house on the west side of Dotwick Street. An Ordnance Survey map dated 1886 indicates that these buildings were superseded by the Clarendon Hotel.

INDUSTRY, COBLE DENE BANK
First recorded in 1850; last recorded in 1855.
Although listed in an 1855 directory as simply the 'Industry', the premises were known as both the Lodge of Industry and the Cottage of Industry. The building overlooked the river Tyne to the south side of Coble Dene Bank. Bearing in mind that during the 1800s, Coble Dene incorporated a lot of heavy shipping industry, the light-hearted names for the pub may have been derived from the busy riverside trades.

KEEL AND FIDDLE, 41 DOTWICK STREET AND DOCK LANE
First recorded in 1822; last recorded in 1834.
The unusual name of this pub probably originates from the freight barges that were used for carrying coal on the river Tyne, along with the violins or 'fiddles' that the keelmen would sometimes play.

KING WILLIAM IV, BRUNSWICK PLACE AND COBLE DENE
First recorded in 1834; last recorded in 1855.
The King William IV stood close to the river Tyne on the north side of Brunswick Place, near the junction with West Row. It was named after William IV, who was king of Great Britain and Ireland (1830–1837), and ascended to the throne after a long naval career; leaving no direct heir, he was succeeded by his niece Victoria.

KINGS ARMS, DUKE STREET
First recorded in 1822; last recorded in 1834.

KINGS HEAD, 34 DUKE STREET
First recorded in 1834; last recorded in 1834.

KINGS HEAD, WALKER PLACE
First recorded in 1827; last recorded in 1827.

LAMB INN, 16/17 DOTWICK STREET
First recorded in 1822; last recorded in 1855.
The Lamb was a small public house situated between the Bee Hive and the Vulcan's Arms on the west side of Dotwick Street.

LETTERS, BULL RING
First recorded in 1822; last recorded in 1822.

LORD BROUGHAM, 21 MIDDLE STREET
First recorded in 1834; last recorded in 1855.
The Lord Brougham stood on the west side of Middle Street, at the corner with Raff Yard, which was a lane connecting North Street and Middle Street. The pub was named after Henry Brougham, who was born in Edinburgh on 19 September 1778. He developed a reputation as a lawyer which brought him to the attention of the leaders of the Whigs.

Brougham was given the task of organising the Whigs' press campaign in the 1807 general election. In 1810 he accepted a parliamentary seat in order to enter the House of Commons. Brougham soon established himself as one of the leading Radicals in Parliament, and he became their spokesman in the House of Commons. In 1830, Brougham was given a peerage and became Lord Chancellor in Lord Grey's new Whig government. Brougham, who had been arguing for parliamentary reform for over thirty years, played an important role in persuading the House of Lords to pass the 1832 Reform Act. Lord Brougham was also one of the main people behind the passing of the 1833 Anti-Slavery Act. He died on 17 May, 1868.

MAGPIE, COBLE DENE
First recorded in 1850; last recorded in 1855.

NEW CLARENDON, APPLEBY STREET
First recorded in 1910; last recorded in 1997.

NORTHUMBERLAND ARMS, 10 NEW QUAY AND MARKET PLACE
First recorded in 1822; last recorded in 1989.
Probably the most famous and widely known of all the licensed premises in North Shields, the Northumberland Arms stood on the New Quay, facing the Old Market Place and river Tyne. Built as a town house for the Duke of Northumberland, the foundation stone of the building which became part of North Shields' market place and incorporated the four-storey Northumberland Arms Hotel was laid on 14 October 1806.

This fine building had two imposing stone pillars at the entrance, above which was the coat of arms of the Duke of Northumberland. It was first sold in 1821, and by 1897, the entire building had been refurbished and redecorated, with the ground floor being redesigned to incorporate new service areas, consisting of a bar, buffet, select room and a dining room. The upper floors contained a large dining room, billiard room, coffee room and smoke rooms designated specifically to cater for the shipbuilding trade. Public functions, luncheons and dinners were held there.

By 1903, the premises had been sold to a Newcastle-upon-Tyne wine and spirit merchants, A.H. Higginbottom & Co, who controlled the premises until the 1920s. The Grade II listed building for many years was better known as 'The Jungle'. It had an international reputation as a magnet for the thousands of hard-living mariners who came ashore here for entertainment. It is believed that it was

The coat of arms on the roof and the pillared porch show the Northumberland Arms (later to be more popularly known as 'The Jungle') in 1912.

nicknamed The Jungle because of the many exotic animal heads and trophies that were displayed in many of the rooms whilst it was in possession of the duke. In 1989, the premises closed, and the building was converted into luxury flats.

PERCY ARMS, WHITEHILL POINT
First recorded in 1850; last recorded in 1855.
This was a large building, situated next to the loading staithes at Whitehill Point, just a few yards away from the edge of the river Tyne.

PERCY MAIN (OLD PERCY MAIN / PERCY MAIN COLLIERY), 28 DOTWICK STREET
First recorded in 1822; last recorded in 1834.

PHOENIX INN, 32/41/42 DUKE STREET AND UNION COURT
First recorded in 1822; last recorded in 1955.
Situated directly opposite the Sussex Arms, the Phoenix Inn, also known as the Phoenix Hotel, stood between Kirby's Bank and Union Court, on the west side of Duke Street, just a little to the south of the Crane House Vaults and the Crown & Thistle. The pub dates back to at least 1850, and was rebuilt in 1902 for Newcastle Breweries. The original idea was to include a long, full-width bar to the front of the site, with a select room and a sitting room to the rear, served by hatches from the bar counter. The plans, however, were modified to make an 'L' shaped bar and make room for the inclusion of a shop so as to earn a rental for the brewery.

PINEAPPLE, 43 DUKE STREET
First recorded in: not recorded; last recorded in: not recorded.

PLOUGH, DOTWICK STREET
First recorded in 1834; last recorded in 1834.

PORTHOLE (REFER TO: GOLDEN FLEECE), 11 NEW QUAY

PRINCE ALBERT, HAYHOLE
First recorded in: not recorded; last recorded in: not recorded.
The exact location of the Prince Albert is unconfirmed, but it was believed to have been situated near the river Tyne in the Hayhole Road area.

QUEENS HEAD, FERRY BOAT LANDING
First recorded in: not recorded; last recorded in: not recorded.

REFORM TAVERN, NORTH STREET
First recorded in 1834; last recorded in 1850.

RISING SUN INN, BRUNSWICK PLACE, BURDON MAIN, ALBERT-EDWARD DOCK, COBLE DENE
First recorded in 1834; last recorded in 1940.
The Rising Sun Inn stood on the north side of Brunswick Place, a few yards to the east of The King William IV public house.

ROSE INN, 4 DENE STREET AND NEW ROW, MOUNT PLEASANT
First recorded in 1834; last recorded in 1940.
The Rose Inn stood on the east side of the road, towards the northern end of Dene Street.

ROYAL ALBERT HOTEL, DENE TERRACE, DENE STREET AND DOCK ROAD
First recorded in 1887; last recorded in 1940.
This hotel was probably named in honour of Albert Edward, the Prince of Wales, who officially opened the nearby dock in 1884, which also came to bear his name. It was situated on Dock Road, at the corner of Dene Terrace and Dene Street.

ROYAL OAK, STEAM MILL LANE, MOUNT PLEASANT
First recorded in 1865; last recorded in 1867.
The Royal Oak was a large public house which stood just off Dotwick Street, at the end of Buckham's Lane near the perimeter of the Mount Pleasant Iron Foundry.

ROYAL QUAYS, COBLE DENE
First recorded in 1996; last recorded in 2007.
Newly built around the historic Albert Edward Dock, and opened in 1884 by Albert Edward, Prince of Wales, the area known as the Royal Quays derives its modern name from this association. Likewise named after the area where it is situated, the Royal Quays public house is a modern building geared towards tourists and families.

SALMON INN, 8/13/22 NORTH STREET AND MILBOURNE PLACE
First recorded in 1822; last recorded in 1920.
The Salmon Inn stood on the east side of North Street, not far from the junction with Brunswick Place.

SHIP, 22 BULL RING
First recorded in 1834; last recorded in 1834.

SHIP, 24/55 MIDDLE STREET
First recorded in 1822; last recorded in 1938.
The Ship Inn stood on the west side of Middle Street, diagonally opposite the Wheatsheaf Inn.

SHIP HOPEWELL, DUKE STREET
First recorded in 1827; last recorded in 1827.

This inn may have been named after the explorer Henry Hudson's first command, the *Hopewell*, which was an aging, 40-ton barque with a small crew. In 1606, John Knight had already sailed the Hopewell in search of the North West Passage along the coast of Labrador. The *Hopewell* was also a ship which carried immigrants from Great Britain to New England in 1634.

STAITH HOUSE, WHITEHILL POINT
First recorded in 1847; last recorded in 1847.

STARLING, 24 SOUTH STREET, EAST STREET AND MILBURN PLACE
First recorded in 1850; last recorded in 1899.
The Starling Inn was a corner building which stood on the north-east apex of East Street, as it curved south into South Street, Mount Pleasant.

STEAM BOAT (REFER TO: FERRY HOUSE), DUKE STREET

STEAM MILL INN, MOUNT PLEASANT
First recorded in 1855; last recorded in 1855.

SUN INN, 7/13 NORTH STREET
First recorded in 1847; last recorded in 1847.

SUSSEX ARMS, 6/34 DUKE STREET
First recorded in 1850; last recorded in 1865.
Situated directly opposite the Phoenix Inn, the Sussex Arms stood on the east side of Duke Street. A narrow alleyway separated it from the tiny Steam Boat public house which stood next door.

THREE MARINERS, DUKE STREET
First recorded in 1822; last recorded in 1827.

TURKS HEAD, 33 DUKE STREET
First recorded in 1822; last recorded in 1930.
The Turks Head stood on the west side of Duke Street, a little to the south of the Crane House Vaults and the Phoenix Inn.

TYNE INN, TENNYSON TERRACE
First recorded in 1938; last recorded in 1938.
This was a small, detached building which stood on Tennyson Terrace.

TYNEMOUTH CASTLE, COLLINGWOOD STREET
First recorded in 1822; last recorded in 1827.

VICTORY, DUKE STREET
First recorded in 1834; last recorded in 1834.

VULCAN'S ARMS, 24 DOTWICK STREET
First recorded in 1850; last recorded in 1855.
The Vulcan's Arms stood directly next door to the Hylton Castle public house on the west side of Dotwick Street. An Ordnance Survey map dated 1886 indicates that these buildings were superseded by the Clarendon Hotel.

Wellington Vaults, *c.* 1935.

WAGON INN, DOTWICK STREET, MILBURN PLACE AND 2 NEW ROW, MOUNT PLEASANT
First recorded in 1822; last recorded in 1912.
The Wagon Inn, originally spelled as 'Waggon', was sited on the north side of a short section of street between the end of Burdon Main Row and Dotwick Street, a little to the east of the Woolsington House Hotel. The area was known as 'Mount Pleasant'.

WELLINGTON VAULTS, 15/17 BULL RING
First recorded in 1865; last recorded in 1940.
The Wellington Vaults stood prominently on the western curve of the Bull Ring, almost opposite the northern end of Dotwick Street.

WHEAT SHEAF, LIMEKILN SHORE
First recorded in 1822; last recorded in 1834.

WHEATSHEAF, 5/7 COLLINGWOOD STREET
First recorded in 1834; last recorded in 1940.
The Wheatsheaf was one of the larger houses in the Bull Ring area, and stood close to the Wellington Vaults, on the north side of Collingwood Street, adjacent to the Black Bull Stairs.

WHEATSHEAF, 20/21 MIDDLE STREET
First recorded in 1855; last recorded in 1912.
The Wheatsheaf stood on the east side of Middle Street, diagonally opposite the Ship Inn.

WOOLSINGTON HOUSE HOTEL, BURDON MAIN ROW, MOUNT PLEASANT
First recorded in 1834; last recorded in 2007 (not trading).
The huge Woolsington House Hotel has existed since at least 1834, and was prominently situated on Burdon Main Row, at the corner with Appleby Street. From the mid-1800s, this area was heavily industrialised, particularly as heavy engineering and ship repairing began to gain momentum. In 1902, the original building was demolished and rebuilt on exactly the same site especially to cater for the expanding commerce in this area of North Shields. The present structure is a large, imposing two-storey red-brick building, and originally consisted of a public bar, buffet, dining room, and a smoke room, and was the local port of call for much of the heavy workforce in the area.

YARMOUTH ARMS, DUKE STREET
First recorded in 1822; last recorded in 1822.

Chapter Four

Percy Main and Chirton

BASS ROCK, FRONT STREET, CHIRTON
First recorded in: not known; last recorded in: not known.

BLUE BELL, CHIRTON LANE, COLLINGWOOD STREET AND WATERVILLA
First recorded in 1822; last recorded in 1834.

BRIG INN, WHITEHOUSE LANE
First recorded in 1958; last recorded in 2006.
The Brig Inn was built in 1958 to accommodate the needs of the then newly built Chirton Grange and Lynn Estates. Despite an extensive refurbishment programme in the early 1990s by Camerons Breweries, the pub, which was situated on Whitehouse Lane at the corner of Sherborne Avenue, ran into a decline during the 1990s and was eventually demolished in 2006.

BROWN COW, HIGH FLATWORTH
First recorded in 1855; last recorded in 1855.
This public house stood immediately behind High Flatworth Farm, on the site of what is now the Tyne Tunnel Trading Estate. It is listed in directories as both the Brown Cow and the Dun Cow.

CANNON, CHIRTON HILL, BILLY MILL
First recorded in 1853; last recorded in c. 1935.
There has been a Cannon Inn recorded at Chirton Hill or Billy Mill since at least 1853. The original Cannon Inn stood to the rear of the present Cannon Inn, directly opposite, and to the west of, the old Billy Windmill, on the edge of Billy Mill Quarry.

CANNON, COAST ROAD, BILLY MILL
First recorded in 1935; last recorded in 2007.
The more familiar modern Cannon Inn was built in 1935, replacing the old pub of the same name which stood nearby. Backing onto Cornhill Crescent, whilst dominating a site on the north side of the Coast Road at Billy Mill, it was built by Benjamin Peel Ltd, a North Shields company. The design is almost identical to the former Collingwood Arms on Front Street and the Spring Gardens Inn on Albion Road. At the time of opening, it was described as a road house with floodlights picking out the walls and porches.

COLLINGWOOD ARMS, 2 FRONT STREET, CHIRTON
First recorded in 1822-1937 (original building); last recorded in 1937-2004 (second building).
Named after Admiral Lord Cuthbert Collingwood, the Northumbrian hero who fought in the Battle of Trafalgar, there has been a Collingwood Arms at Chirton since at least 1822. Rebuilt in 1937 for

Left: The Brig under demolition in 2006.

Below: The Collingwood Arms, Chirton, taken from the original architectural plans.

Newcastle Breweries to replace the former Collingwood Arms which stood nearby, it was built by Benjamin Peel Ltd of North Shields in the same style as the Cannon Inn, Billy Mill and Spring Gardens Inn, Albion Road. The pub, being no longer viable, closed its doors for the last time in 2004, before being demolished to make way for a sheltered housing project. It stood on the corner of Front Street, Chirton at its junction with Billy Mill Avenue.

HOPEWELL COLLIERY, CHIRTON
First recorded in 1822; last recorded in 1879.
Named after the Hopewell Colliery, which at one time stood on the area of land between the old Ralph Gardner School and Waterville Road, this pub was also referred to as the Hopewell Pit. The exact location of this pub has not been established, and there is no available information about it.

Station Road, Percy Main, looking north *c.* 1912. The Percy Arms can be seen to the extreme left of the picture.

MILL, CHIRTON
First recorded in 1834; last recorded in 1834.

NAUTILUS, 191 VERNE ROAD
First recorded in 1961; last recorded in 2007.
Built in 1961, the Nautilus pub derived its name from the street on which it stands – Verne Road. The connection is slightly cryptic: in 1870, the French writer Jules Verne wrote the science fiction novel *20,000 Leagues under the Sea*, in which the submarine commanded by Captain Nemo was called the *Nautilus*. The connection between the names Verne and Nautilus should therefore be obvious!

PERCY ARMS, STATION ROAD, PERCY MAIN
First recorded in 1835; last recorded in 2007.
The Percy Arms has existed since at least 1853, and in those days was situated opposite High Row, immediately next to the tracks of the old Seaton Burn Colliery waggonway. Today, it is better described as standing close to the Metro Bridge, slightly to the north of Percy Main station, on Station Road.

PHOENIX, PHOENIX CHASE, NEW YORK
First recorded in 1977; last recorded in 2003.
The Phoenix was a modern-style pub built for Camerons Breweries, and had a very short lifespan. Regular breaches of licensing laws were addressed by the police, and the pub was in a location where it suffered frequent attacks of vandalism, soon falling into a state of disrepair. As a result the pub closed down and was demolished in 2003.

PINEAPPLE INN, 78 WALLSEND ROAD, CHIRTON
First recorded in 1787; last recorded in 2007.
John Dobson, the great northern architect, was born in 1787 at 'the Pine Apple Inn'. The inn at this time had a large fruit garden, with convenient seating, and accommodation for guests and parties, and landlord was Dobson's father. Chirton was regarded as a fashionable resort during the summer months, with mansions, cottages and quaint flower gardens.

The Pineapple Inn, *c.* 1950.

REDBURN, WATERVILLE ROAD AND WALLSEND ROAD
First recorded in 1956; last recorded in 2007.

St John's vicarage was built in around 1871 on the apex of Wallsend Road and Waterville Lane, but by the early 1950s had been vacated as such. In 1956, this fine, stone-built house was purchased and extensive internal work commenced in order to convert it into a public house. During this time, a beautiful wooden spiral staircase was removed, and the old cellar was fitted with refrigeration equipment to accommodate the storage of beer and ales. The house took the name 'The Redburn' because of a nearby stream known as the Red Burn. It officially opened as a pub on the 18 December 1956.

RIDGES INN, WATERVILLE ROAD
First recorded in 1940-1969 as the Ridges Inn; last recorded in 1969-2007 as the Seine Boat.

The Ridges Estate was built on land which was at one time part of Ridges Farm, and was specifically designed and built to rehouse the large number of people displaced during the clearance of the Dockwray Square and riverside slums during the 1930s. As the Ridges Estate grew, its population had increased to almost 10,000, and it was agreed that there was a need for a public house in the area, which was built in 1939 and styled 'the Ridges Inn' after the name of the estate.

The Redburn, *c.* 1950.

The inn was built by Benjamin Peel Ltd of North Shields for William McEwan & Co. Ltd, and comprised three large public drinking rooms, a bar, a sitting room, a buffet and an off-sale shop. The inn opened for business in the early years of the Second World War, on the 16 April 1940. By the 1960s, Tynemouth Council were concerned that the name of the Ridges Estate had developed a social stigma, and in 1969, the entire estate was renamed the Meadowell (from a well that was situated in the corner of a nearby field), recognised as Meadowell Farm.

The council approached the owners of the Ridges Inn, which at that time was Scottish & Newcastle Breweries, with a plea to change the pub name. Two names were suggested: 'The Meadow' or 'The Robins' (in honour of North Shields' football team, who were known as the Robins). Neither name was favoured: 'The Robins', it was felt, might have been confused with the nearby Robin Hood Inn. Eventually, the pub was renamed simply as the 'Seine Boat', to reflect the nearby fishing industry.

ROBIN HOOD, 4 FRONT STREET/78 WALLSEND ROAD, CHIRTON
First recorded in 1822-1959 (old building); last recorded in 1959-2007 (new building).
Named after the legendary folk hero who is reputed to have lived in Sherwood Forest, there have been two 'Robin Hood' inns at Chirton. The first inn was demolished in 1959, and stood next to the present building, which was built the same year. A newspaper advertising feature dated 1959 indicates that the new pub comprised three bars, a buffet and a sitting room.

SEINE BOAT (REFER TO: RIDGES INN), WATERVILLE ROAD

Chapter Five

Preston Township

ALEXANDRA, QUEEN ALEXANDRA ROAD
First recorded in 1965; last recorded in 2007.
The Alexandra was built in 1965 and is situated not far from the junction with Hawkeys Lane, on the south side of Queen Alexandra Road. This street was named after the consort of Edward VII, Queen Alexandra (1844-1925). The pub's name is simply an abbreviated version of the road it stands on.

BAMBURGH CASTLE, FRONT STREET, PRESTON
First recorded in 1834; last recorded in 1938.
The first record of the Bamburgh Castle appears in Pigots' 1834 Directory, and subsequent directories have shown different spellings of the name, which include: Bambro, Bamborough, and Bambrough. The inn stood next door to the Spread Eagle Inn, on the site of what is now the car-parking area beside Popplewell Terrace. In 1937, the Chief Constable of Tynemouth, Tom Blackburn, expressed concerns over the hygiene condition of the premises, and as a result he refused to renew the licence on the grounds that there were already two other satisfactory premises in the village, referring to both the Spread Eagle and the Sportsman. As a result, the Bamburgh Castle closed down. The building became derelict and was demolished in the early 1960s.

BOARD, SOUTH PRESTON
First recorded in 1847; last recorded in 1847.

DUN COW, PRESTON
First recorded in 1822; last recorded in 1834.
The location of an inn by this name in Preston Village or Preston Township has not been established, but it is likely that the directory reference has been confused with that of the Dun Cow at New York Village, which lies not far from the old Preston Township boundary.

FOXHUNTERS INN, NORTH ROAD, PRESTON
First recorded in 1834; last recorded in 1938.
The Foxhunters originally stood next to Preston Gardens, at Preston Gate, on the site which now forms the junction of Preston Road and North Road. Although this is unconfirmed, it is believed to have been called 'The Plane Tree' sometime prior to 1834, when the then landlord, Thomas Craig, renamed the pub 'The Foxhunters Inn' after his passion for hunting. In later years, part of the premises were converted to a small shop, and in 2006, it once again underwent a number of alterations to convert it into a house, where many of the original external features and building characteristics are still evident. The inn ceased trading in 1939, when the owners, Newcastle Breweries, decided to close it and replace it with the new Foxhunters Inn, which was built half a mile to the north, at the junction of Preston North Road and Rake Lane.

Preston Road in 1901, showing the first Foxhunters Inn.

FOXHUNTERS INN, RAKE LANE/PRESTON NORTH ROAD, PRESTON
First recorded in 1939; last recorded in 2007.
When the original Foxhunters Inn at Preston Village closed, it was replaced by the new Foxhunters Inn, which was built on a prominent corner site in 1939 at the Rake Lane junction with Preston North Road where it still stands to this day. Over the years, the pub has undergone several refurbishments and alterations, and is now geared towards catering for families with the restaurant and food market. being the main priority.

GUNNER, PRESTON ROAD
First recorded in 1963; last recorded in 2007.
Constructed in 1963, and opened in 1964, The Gunner is a relatively modern public house, occupying a prominent corner site on the east side of Preston Road at its junction with Trevor Terrace. The original intention was to name this pub 'The Green Jacket'; however, after a last-minute decision, it was decided to name it 'The Gunner' because of Tynemouth's long association with the Royal Regiment of Artillery. The opening ceremony was performed on 7 July 1964 by Sir Robert Younger, president of Scottish & Newcastle Breweries.

HALF MOON, PRESTON LANE
First recorded in 1822; last recorded in 1828.
There is no information available about this inn, which is listed only in early directories as standing on Preston Lane, with a licensee by the name of John Hedley.

MAGIC LANTERN, PRESTON NORTH ROAD
First recorded in 1999; last recorded in 2007.
Situated on the west side of Preston North Road, North Shields, as part of Preston Grange Estate, the Magic Lantern was built in 1999 and replaced the previous pub which stood nearby – The Pheasant. It was built on an area of land which had previously been part of the Grangeway Shopping Centre. The Magic Lantern is mainly food-orientated and is a typical modern building catering for families.

Cawthorn Terrace in around 1920, and preparations for an outing from the Sportsman.

ORANGE TREE, PRESTON LANE
First recorded in 1822; last recorded in 1834.
It is often thought that this inn may have been the same premises as the nearby Foxhunters Inn, also listed in Preston. However, this is unlikely as there are separate listings in Pigots' 1834 directory showing different landlords for each inn. This suggests that these would have been two different premises. In 1834, the landlord of the Orange Tree was shown as a James Hogg, who also owned some nearby nursery gardens which stood on the site of the present West Dene Drive. Little else is known about this pub.

PHEASANT, PRESTON NORTH ROAD
First recorded in 1972; last recorded in 1999.
As a building, this public house has had a very short lifespan; built in 1972 to accommodate the residents of Preston Grange Estate, it fell into decline with the nearby shopping centre, and was demolished less than thirty years later in 1999. It was replaced by a newer and larger pub which took the name of the Magic Lantern.

SPORTSMAN, FRONT STREET, PRESTON
First recorded in 1814; last recorded in 2007.
Although at one time referred to as the Sportsman's Arms, the Sportsman probably derived its name from its close association with Preston Races (sometimes referred to as Preston Hoppings) which finished close to the public house. The pub has stood on this site since at least 1814, when it was owned by a Mr John Fenwick, who also owned much of the land in Preston Township. By 1895, the

The Spread Eagle, c. 1966.

premises came into the possession of Mr William Cawthorn, who in 1896 submitted an application to carry out a full renovation of the building, with the frontage being given a complete facelift to take on a Tudor-style design, which it still bears to this day. William Cawthorn gave his name to the row of houses on the east side of the pub, namely Cawthorn Terrace.

SPREAD EAGLE, FRONT STREET, PRESTON
First recorded in 1822; last recorded in 2007.
The Spread Eagle is situated on the south side of Front Street, Preston Village between Preston Road and Popplewell Terrace. Early alteration work is evident, as it is known that during the early 1900s, the original sandstone frontage was rendered with cement and the front door was repositioned. Further internal alterations were carried out during the 1970s, which included a full refit, replacing the very small bar, sitting room and 'bottle and jug' with an open-plan aspect. With the exception of an extension which was added to the west side of the building in 2005, the main structure remains as one of the oldest buildings in the village. The popular, informal term 'Spread Eagle' is derived from a heraldic depiction of an eagle displayed with wings, body and legs outspread and visible, which has been used as the emblem of a number of states and monarchs.

WHITE LION, PRESTON
First recorded in 1822; last recorded in 1822.
In 1822, Daniel Hogg is recorded as the licensee of the White Lion, but the exact location of this inn has not been established. It is likely however, that it was sited on part of one of the local market gardens owned by the Hogg family who had nursery gardens in the area. Little else is known of the premises.

Chapter Six

Tynemouth

BARCAS (REFER TO: BATH HOTEL), THE ARCADE/12 BATH TERRACE,
TYNEMOUTH

BATH INN / BATH HOTEL, THE ARCADE/12 BATH TERRACE, TYNEMOUTH
First recorded in 1822; last recorded in 2007.
Originally an eighteenth-century coaching inn, the three-storey Bath Hotel, (later to become the
Royal Sovereign and Furry Pear), took its name from the nearby nineteenth-century baths, which
were situated below the priory at Priors Haven.

In 1820, the proprietor was a Mrs Hannah Spurrier, who monopolised most of the bathing
machines at Tynemouth. Shows and plays were performed there from 1821 to 1826. In 1860,
the arcade was covered in, and in 1869, the Bath Assembly Rooms were built on the opposite
side, with a reading room and racquet court adjoining to the east. This part of the building
incorporates what became Oz's and Bertie's Bar in the 1990s, and more recently, Barcas. By 1887,
the Bath Hotel contained a small bar and snug room, along with a large dining room, coffee room,
and guest rooms, and traditionally catered for much of Tynemouth's tourist trade. By 1910, the
assembly rooms were detached from the hotel, and remained in use until the 1960s as banqueting
rooms.

After the Second World War, Newcastle Breweries took over the premises, and in 1967, part of the
premises were converted to become 'the Royal Sovereign', named after Admiral Lord Collingwood's
ship at the Battle of Trafalgar. Alteration work over the years saw this name change again to 'the Furry
Pear', and subsequently to 'Blue'.

BAXTERS, FRONT STREET, TYNEMOUTH
First recorded in 1968; last recorded in 2007.
One of the newer establishments in Tynemouth village was The Baxter, the origins of its name being
taken from the long-established Baxters Café and Tea Rooms, which stood on the site up until 1968.
The pub was established by Sir John Fitzgerald Ltd, and remodelled some years later to become better
known as Fitzpatricks.

BLUE (REFER TO: BATH HOTEL), THE ARCADE/12 BATH TERRACE, TYNEMOUTH

BROADWAY, THE BROADWAY, TYNEMOUTH
First recorded in 1962; last recorded in 2007.
Occupying a large site at the junction of The Broadway and Beach Road, The Broadway pub was
built in 1962. The pub has been extensively modernised and extended over the years, latterly taking
up a large part of the floor space to concentrate on the provision of food with a restaurant area.

A quiet Front Street in 1909. The Cumberland Arms is the building to the left, and the Salutation is the white building in the centre of the picture.

BULL AND DOG, 52 FRONT STREET, TYNEMOUTH
First recorded in 1822; last recorded in 1834.
The first record of the Bull and Dog dates to 1822, but by 1877, the premises were better known as the Percy Arms.

BULMERS TEMPERANCE HOTEL AND EATING HOUSE, PERCY STREET, TYNEMOUTH
First recorded in 1877; last recorded in 1877.
Little seems to be recorded for this establishment; however, a newspaper advertisement of 1877 indicates that the premises were situated at the foot of Percy Street.

CUMBERLAND ARMS, 17 FRONT STREET, TYNEMOUTH
First recorded in 1855; last recorded in 2007.
Situated on the north side of Front Street, the exterior of the Cumberland Arms remains virtually unaltered from when it was first constructed. The appearance results from three periods of building, in 1898, 1934 and the early 1960s. The frontage consists of three striking ogee archways, which frame a central window, and two doors. There is a decorative cornice; above is a faience panel of glazed brick that incorporates the name of the pub. The building stands on a long, narrow site, and originally consisted of a front public bar, with a select bar or sitting room, a 'bottle and jug', and a rear smoke room. Access to the rear of the pub was (and still is) possible via an external alleyway.

The rear of the pub sits on an elevated level, and one of the unusual features of the original building was an octagonal buffet room on the upper rear floor. This was demolished in 1934 during a phase of some internal alterations. A first-floor club room was also replaced by private accommodation. In the early 1960s, the Cumberland Arms became part of the Scottish & Newcastle Breweries' estate, and the company carried out major alterations to the interior, removing all of the remaining internal partition

East Street, Tynemouth, *c.* 1885. The Gibraltar Rock is the prominent white building in the centre of the photograph.

walls, and introduced a nautical theme, making use of the different levels that existed between the front bar and rear buffet to create an 'upper deck' and a 'lower deck'. The front bar's counter remains virtually unchanged, and is still in the same place as it was in 1898.

DOLPHIN INN, SPITAL HILL, SPITAL DENE AND KING EDWARD ROAD, TYNEMOUTH
First recorded in 1834; last recorded in 2007.
The Dolphin Inn is situated on the north side of King Edward Road, Tynemouth, on the area formerly called Spital Hill. This is a popular name for several British public houses, and such inns are usually located in coastal areas where the dolphin was, naturally, a popular symbol.

FITZPATRICKS (REFER TO: BAXTERS), FRONT STREET, TYNEMOUTH

FURRY PEAR (REFER TO: BATH HOTEL), THE ARCADE/12 BATH TERRACE, TYNEMOUTH

GIBRALTAR ROCK, 3 EAST STREET, TYNEMOUTH
First recorded in 1822; last recorded in 2007.
The Gibraltar Rock public house is situated at the south end of East Street, Tynemouth and sits high on the cliff tops which overlook both King Edward's Bay and Benebal Crag, on which the priory and castle are located. The original Gibraltar Rock Inn dates to at least 1822: however, the inn which we know today is actually a combination of two inns and cottages which stood on the site for over 100 years until 1927. The Priory Inn stood slightly to the north of the original Gibraltar Rock, separated by the cottages, and these buildings were later converted to the Gibraltar Rock that we know today. When Bass Breweries took over the pub in 1964, major internal renovation and modernisation work was carried out. However, the exterior rendered stonework has remained largely unaltered.

GRAND HOTEL, SEA BANKS AND PERCY GARDENS, TYNEMOUTH
First recorded in 1872; last recorded in 2007.

The Grand Hotel is an imposing building situated at the end of Percy Gardens, Tynemouth, overlooking the North Sea. Owned by the Duke of Northumberland, and initially built as a summer residence in 1872 for the Duchess, it was converted to a hotel in 1877. Throughout its chequered past the Grand Hotel has always been regarded as the most luxurious hotel in the area, with one of its main attractions being the opulent sweeping staircase, reminiscent of the Victorian period when such grand buildings were used to host balls for the aristocracy.

During its lifetime it has played host to innumerable colourful characters from the worlds of stage, cinema, politics and sport; it has survived two world wars, the 1930s Depression and constant changes of ownership, and yet still remains proud and majestic. One of the best-known managers was a Thomas Tickle, who came to the Grand Hotel in the late 1890s and at one time was responsible for running both the Grand and the Bath Hotel in nearby Tynemouth village. He was a highly respected manager: the customers liked him and it was obvious he enjoyed his job because he died whilst playing billiards in the hotel with one of the locals.

The Victorian period helped make Tynemouth village popular, with tourists flocking to this small seaside resort, keen to indulge in its delightful climate and explore its natural beauty. Tynemouth was, for a time, a spa town. When, in 1912, it was recorded that the death rate in Tynemouth was the lowest in the kingdom as a result of its spa waters, such news was greeted with an influx of visitors. Businesses and local hotels thrived: this was the publicity they needed to lure people to visit and even the Grand saw fit to advertise in the local press of the time as having 'twenty-eight bedrooms, bathrooms and liveries, hot and cold water and salt supplies'. Never had Tynemouth or the Grand Hotel been so busy.

Sadly the First World War took its toll on the Grand: battered and bruised, a mere skeleton of its former self, stripped of all its glory and finesse, it was another helpless victim of a needless war. At that time Tynemouth village was overrun with young recruits billeted at the barracks whilst their commanding officers were accommodated in the Grand Hotel. After a heavy day on duty, the officers indulged in a heavy night of drinking and playing billiards, and so when the war ended and the officers eventually left, the Grand was in such a state of disrepair that it had to be closed down and completely refurbished. As a result the hotel did not re-open to the public until 1922. It took a lot of hard work for the Grand to become re-established and restored to its former glory, with large amounts of money spent on redecorating and repairing the damage the officers had left behind.

Staff employed at the Grand have always taken great pride in their work. Even at a time when the entrance stairs were often scrubbed twice daily and the woodwork polished until shining, working fourteen hour shifts – sometimes seven days a week – for a mere 4s a week was not unusual. The work was hard. Staff were frequently so weary after a shift that they fell into bed out of sheer exhaustion, but it was steady employment that provided them with a roof over their heads and guaranteed food in their stomachs at a time when many people were barely making a living.

There are few hotels in the North East that can admit to having entertained so many celebrities of screen and stage. It became quite a regular occurrence for staff to see familiar faces coming down the staircase for breakfast: such celebrities and much-loved people as Mike and Bernie Winters, Stanley Baker, Margaret Rutherford and Conservative MP for Tynemouth Dame Irene Ward, a much celebrated visitor to the Grand and noted for the variety of hats she would wear. Irish comedian Dave Allen was a guest, as was Dame Vera Lynn – and yet, for most people, the most famous were comedy duo Stan Laurel and Oliver Hardy, who would make a point of staying at the Grand Hotel whenever they were appearing at the Theatre Royal in Newcastle. For Stan it was a case of coming home, as he had spent the early part of his childhood living in North Shields.

Hotspur Street in 1911, and the magnificent Grand Hotel.

By the 1950s the Grand Hotel was beginning to return to its former beauty, with extensive restoration work having taken a great deal of time and money on the part of the owners. It was also in the late 1950s that the Grand welcomed another new manager: Mr Bright, his wife and their two young daughters from Lagos. Apparently he was quite a distinguished gentleman, towering over 6ft tall whilst his wife, of Welsh descent and somewhat smaller in stature, ruled the roost with a firm hand: a compatible pair, feared, yet respected. With each new manager came new ideas on how to attract more customers. It was the Brights' innovative idea to open the Troll Bar in the basement of the Hotel (and have it decorated by two Newcastle Art College students), which at the time was considered very fashionable, especially at weekends when it staged live music. Adjoining the hotel on Hotspur Street was the Clachan Bar, later to become known as Copperfields Bar. In recent years, the hotel has undergone much refurbishment work, restoring all to its former Victorian splendour, and for many people the hotel still holds many cherished memories.

GREENLAND FISHERY, 18 BACK STREET, TYNEMOUTH
First recorded in 1834; last recorded in 1834.
Another public house of the same name existed on Charlotte Street, North Shields: however, the reason behind such a strange name for a pub in Tynemouth where there was little or no connection with the fishing trade remains a mystery.

NEWCASTLE ARMS, 20 FRONT STREET, TYNEMOUTH
First recorded in 1834; last recorded in 1834.

NORTHUMBERLAND ARMS, PERCY SQUARE AND PERCY TERRACE, TYNEMOUTH
First recorded in 1822; last recorded in 1855.
The Northumberland Arms was a large building which stood adjacent to Tynemouth Road, opposite the Master Mariner's Asylum. Situated in its own grounds, at the south-east corner of Percy Square, this is the area which is now occupied by the Sir James Knott Memorial Flats.

ORDNANCE ARMS, CASTLE YARD, TYNEMOUTH
First recorded in 1855; last recorded in 1855.
Because of its location within Tynemouth Castle grounds, it is likely that this name was chosen because of the early military connection. Little is known or recorded in relation to this pub.

OZ'S BAR (REFER TO: BATH HOTEL), THE ARCADE /12 BATH TERRACE, TYNEMOUTH

PARK HOTEL, GRAND PARADE, TYNEMOUTH
First recorded in 1938; last recorded in 2007.
Built in 1938, the Park Hotel occupies a prominent situation on the seafront junction with Beach Road, overlooking Tynemouth Long Sands. The building was designed in the Art Deco style by J.R. Wallace, a Newcastle-upon-Tyne architect, and built by Hastie D. Burton, a long established North Shields construction company. Originally consisting of thirty rooms and two suites, much of the hotel has since been altered, enlarged and extended over the years, not all of which is in keeping with the original 1930s style.

PERCY ARMS, 25/60 FRONT STREET, TYNEMOUTH
First recorded in 1834; last recorded in 2007.
The original Percy Arms, on Front Street, has existed since the mid-1830s, and stood on the same site as the present building. It was originally a plain-fronted three-storey brick building. It was rebuilt in 1931 with a bar, lounge bar, select room, and a mixed room. The building, however, did not extend around the corner into Hotspur Street until after rebuilding work was completed. Extensive alterations were carried out during the early 1960s, and again in the late 1990s, where the entire ground floor was converted to form an open-plan aspect.

PRIORY INN, BANK TOP AND 5 EAST STREET, TYNEMOUTH
First recorded in 1855; last recorded in 1924.
The Priory Inn was a small inn which was situated on East Street, Tynemouth a few yards to the north of the original Gibraltar Rock Inn, overlooking King Edward's Bay. The pub closed in 1924; however, in 1927, the building was converted to incorporate the Gibraltar Rock that we know today.

PRUDHOE HOTEL (REFER TO: SHIPWRIGHTS ARMS), 18 PERCY STREET, TYNEMOUTH

QUEENS HEAD, 45 FRONT STREET, TYNEMOUTH
First recorded in 1834; last recorded in 1834.

ROSE OF ALLENDALE, 8 PERCY STREET, TYNEMOUTH
First recorded in 1855; last recorded in 1924.
The delightfully named Rose of Allendale was one of four public houses on Percy Street, and stood on the north side of the road, halfway between Silver Street and East Street. The pub closed down in 1924, and is now a private dwelling house.

The original Percy Arms, Front Street, Tynemouth, *c. 1925.*

ROYAL HOTEL, OXFORD STREET, TYNEMOUTH
First recorded in 1855; last recorded in 1887

ROYAL SOVEREIGN (REFER TO: BATH HOTEL), THE ARCADE/12 BATH TERRACE, TYNEMOUTH

SALUTATION INN, 16/62 FRONT STREET, TYNEMOUTH
First recorded in 1790; last recorded in 2007.
Early in the thirteenth century, when the present Tynemouth Priory was under construction, the monks had gardens where they grew herbs to make medicine for the poor people. The monks had a brew house where they produced various ales, and the younger monks had to learn the secret of brewing the herbs, extracting the virtue to make it ready for use. The sign of the inn belonging to Tynemouth Priory would have been 'The Salutation', bearing witness to the days when the monasteries were actively concerned in the ownership and control of many English inns, the sign of which was an illustration of the Angel Gabriel saluting the Virgin Mary. Wayfarers, pilgrims and knights travelling the coast would drink at the inn, which would help pay for the building of the priory.

The Salutation, Front Street, *c.* 1920.

It is likely that the present Salutation Inn, standing on the south side of Front Street, dates back to 1790 and took its name from these times. Originally a coaching inn, converted from two separate houses, there was sufficient stabling for up to twenty-four horses, with the interior consisting of a front bar, and four small sitting rooms. Despite modernisations over the years, followed by extensive interior alterations in 1964, much of the exterior of the building is still in its original format.

SAMMY JACK'S, FRONT STREET, TYNEMOUTH
First recorded in 2000; last recorded in 2007.
Situated on the south-east corner of Front Street and Colbeck Terrace, the former Tynemouth Congregational church of 1868 fell into disuse during the 1960s and 1970s, and was converted to an indoor shopping mall, adopting the name of 'The Land of Green Ginger'. Another part of the same church buildings facing onto Front Street was taken over by local businessman Mr James Sample, who converted the premises to a pub which he named after a family member – Sammy Jack.

SEVEN STARS, 12 BACK STREET AND 15 PERCY STREET, TYNEMOUTH
First recorded in 1822; last recorded in 1924.
The Seven Stars was one of the largest public houses in Tynemouth village. It stood on the north side of Percy Street, directly opposite the end of Silver Street. It was closed as a pub in 1924, and converted to a private dwelling house.

SHIPWRIGHTS ARMS, 15 BACK STREET/18 PERCY STREET, TYNEMOUTH
First recorded in 1822-1875 as the Shipwrights Arms; last recorded in 1875-1924 as the
Prudhoe Hotel.

As Tynemouth had little connection with the shipbuilding industry, it seems unusual to have a pub by the name of the Shipwrights Arms in the village. It stood on the north side of Back Street, (a continuation of Percy Street), Tynemouth, and as one of four public houses on this street, it was situated between the Seven Stars and the Union Tavern. (The other pub was the Rose of Allendale). Some time after 1875, the Shipwrights Arms was renamed the Prudhoe Hotel and renumbered as 18 Percy Street. It closed down as a public house in 1924, and was demolished in 1926 to allow the extension of Hotspur Street to connect with Front Street.

STAR AND GARTER HOTEL, 7 FRONT STREET AND 7 MANOR ROAD, TYNEMOUTH
First recorded in 1821; last recorded in 1865.

The Star and Garter Hotel was a large double-fronted building, which stood on the north side of Tynemouth Front Street, on the section that was later to be renamed Manor Road. In 1866, the *Shields Daily News* included an auction sale notice praising the building as, 'A First Class Hotel, occupying the finest possible position and covering an extensive area in that most popular of Northern watering places – Tynemouth'. The notice indicated that the sale was to be held at six o'clock on the evening of Tuesday 2 October 1866, and describes the Star and Garter as follows:

PRINCIPAL FLOOR; A large front Coffee Room or Dining Parlour, exceedingly comfortable with a noble Bay Window, The 'Star', a pleasant Front Room, also with a Bay Window, the well-frequented Smoking Rooms, The 'Haven' and 'Cove', Capital Bar, Waiters' Pantry, Larder, Cupboards &c.

FIRST FLOOR; Two delightful Parlours, the 'Crown' and the 'Sceptre', with Folding Partition, removable at pleasure, and forming one very large and beautiful Assembly Room: Two Cheerful Bedrooms: Small Sitting Room and Chambermaids Closet with Water Closet on Landing.

SECOND FLOOR; Six Airy Bedrooms, the rooms just enumerated are approached by the principal Staircase. A secondary Staircase leads to Nine other Bedrooms, Sitting Room, well-lighted Corridor with Water Closet on Landing &c. To the rear of the Premises are capital Tea and Cooking Kitchens, fitted with Metal Ranges &c., Coal Store, Flagged Yard, Boot House, Laundry and Hay Loft, Water Closet &c. In the Basement are excellent Wine, Ale and Beer Cellars of first-rate temperature.

This splendid Hotel, of a handsome exterior and possessing an air of superiority, is situated almost in the centre of the much admired and greatly frequented watering Place of Tynemouth. Its internal accommodation is complete and fully commensurate to the requirements of a First Class Hotel. It has long enjoyed an Aristocratic Patronage, and must daily increase in value and importance. There is a splendid sea view towards the North. Of Tynemouth it would be superfluous to enlarge. Its beautiful position on the coast and its many interesting features combine to make it the most fashionable Watering Place in the North.

It is unfortunate that there are no records of the auction which indicate what the sale of the hotel realised. After its discontinued use as a hotel, the building reverted to use as a private house, the address of which is now 7 Manor Road.

The Star and Garter Hotel, 7 Front Street, Tynemouth.

TURKS HEAD HOTEL, 41/64 FRONT STREET, TYNEMOUTH
First recorded in 1827; last recorded in 2007.

The Turks Head is a fine three-storey building which has stood on the north side of Front Street, Tynemouth since at least 1778, when there is a record of it having been sold for the sum of £6,000. During the 1800s, the ground-floor bar ran almost the entire length of the building from front to back, with a bar, snug, smoke and billiard rooms on the first floor. The top floor contained a dining room.

Alterations carried out in 1905 saw the ground-floor bar converted to include three sections, which comprised a rear sitting room, along with two 'bottle and jugs'. At one time, the first floor was adorned with an ironwork balcony, and the white glazed faience, covering all three floors of the building, was added during modernisation work carried out in the late 1930s. Since that time, the interior of the hotel has undergone many other changes; however, the exterior has largely remained unaltered.

Locally, the Turks Head is referred to as 'the Stuffed Dog', because of its connections with the local folklore tale of the collie known as 'Wandering Willie', who stands preserved in a glass case in the hallway of the pub.

TYNEMOUTH LODGE HOTEL, 3 CORRECTION HOUSE BANK AND 3 TYNEMOUTH ROAD, TYNEMOUTH

First recorded in 1799; last recorded in 2007.

The Tynemouth Lodge Hotel stands on Correction House Bank, (a part of Tynemouth Road, almost opposite the top of Tanners Bank). The pub has past links with the old House of Correction building next door, which loaned its name to the steep bank on which it is situated. At one time, meals were prepared in Tynemouth Lodge for the prisoners held in the House of Correction, and were delivered there via a tunnel from the cellar. Tynemouth Lodge is one of a small number of public houses in the area which has retained the original glazed terracotta faience as well as the original pub signage above the windows and entrance.

UNION TAVERN, 24 PERCY STREET, TYNEMOUTH

First recorded in 1855; last recorded in 1924.

The Union Tavern stood on the north side of Back Street, (a continuation of Percy Street), Tynemouth, and was one of four public houses on this street. It stood on the site of what is now the north-western corner of Percy Street and Hotspur Street. An article in an early licensing register relating to the Union Tavern provides some interesting information, showing distances to other licensed houses in the vicinity:

Distance from the Union Tavern to: the Prudhoe Hotel: 31 yards.
Distance from the Union Tavern to: the Seven Stars: 45 yards.
Distance from the Union Tavern to: the Rose of Allendale: 92 yards.
Distance from the Union Tavern to: the Priory Inn: 165 yards.
Distance from the Union Tavern to: the Cumberland Arms: 152 yards.
Distance from the Union Tavern to: the Percy Arms: 91 yards.
Distance from the Union Tavern to: the Salutation: 167 yards.

The Union Tavern closed in 1924.

Chapter Seven

Whitley Bay

AVENUE HOTEL, PARK AVENUE, WHITLEY BAY
First recorded in 1907; last recorded in 2007.
The Avenue Hotel was at one time one of the largest hotels in Whitley Bay, occupying a prominent situation on the seafront, at the southern corner with Park Avenue. It was originally built in 1907 as a temperance hotel, and in later years catered for much of Whitley Bay's holiday trade. Internally there were recreation rooms, a large dining hall, tea rooms, and a large lounge with a dance floor, with drawing rooms, smoke rooms and bedrooms on the upper floors, which were later extended south, to bridge the rear lane of Park Avenue onto Brook Street, and forming an annexe for the hotel.

In 1921, the Avenue was granted a licence to sell and serve alcohol, but following a fall in trade, it became a public house some years later, leaving much of the former hotel section lying empty. The public house eventually closed, and the premises were vacated in the early years of this century, falling into a state of disrepair.

BEDROOM (REFER TO: WHITLEY PARK INN), WHITLEY ROAD, WHITLEY BAY

BERKELEY TAVERN, MARINE AVENUE, WHITLEY BAY
First recorded in c. 1930; last recorded in 2007.
Originally constructed as a café, the Berkeley Tavern stands on the north side of Marine Avenue, near to the seafront. During the early 1950s it was known as the Berkeley Restaurant and was a popular venue during the holiday season, particularly Glasgow Fair week during the 1950s and 1960s. The early 1960s saw the Berkeley change from a restaurant to a public house, where it soon became a popular venue and meeting place for motorcycle enthusiasts right up to the mid-1980s, with meetings, dances, discos, parties and social functions being held most evenings in the upstairs rooms.

BRIAR DENE (REFER TO: CULVERT INN), THE LINKS, WHITLEY BAY

CROWN & THISTLE, HILLHEADS ROAD, WHITLEY HILL HEADS
First recorded in 1815; first recorded in 1927.
The Crown & Thistle was situated about a hundred yards to the west of the present Railway Inn (now called 'Last Orders'). It was later renamed and became the first Railway Inn, probably after the nearby Whitley Waggonway, which crossed Hillheads Road next to where the pub stood at that time. During the latter years of the old pub, John Dawson, of Whitley Bay ran the premises. He was married to an Esther Emerson of Wearhead.

The Avenue Hotel at its peak in 1912.

CULVERT INN, THE LINKS, WHITLEY BAY
First recorded in 1887–1906 as the Culvert Inn; last recorded in 1906–2007 as the
Briardene.
The Culvert Inn was situated on the west side of Whitley Links, on part of the estate belonging to
Lord Hastings. Over the years, many alterations have been made to the original building to form what
is now the present Briardene, which was renamed as such in 1906 because of its close proximity to
the local beauty spot of the same name. Strictly speaking, the name is incorrectly spelled and should
really be Brier Dene, as all the early Ordnance Survey maps and documents show this as the definitive
spelling. Briar Dene is in fact a modern corruption of the old name.

ESPLANADE HOTEL, ESPLANADE AND PROMENADE, WHITLEY BAY
First recorded in 1892; last recorded in 2007.
The definition of the word esplanade is: 'A flat open stretch of pavement or grass, especially one
designed as a promenade along a shore'. Located on the seafront overlooking the sea, and built on the
corner of streets named 'The Promenade' and 'The Esplanade', the origin and reason for the name of
this hotel becomes obvious. Built in 1892, the hotel underwent extensive refurbishment in 1922 and
again in 1948, and during the 1980s part of the hotel was transformed into separate theme-bar areas
catering primarily for weekend nightlife, and adopted the names 'Idols' and the 'Lazi Pig'.

FAT OX, FRONT STREET AND PARK VIEW, WHITLEY BAY
First recorded in 1822; last recorded in 2007.
The Fat Ox is situated on the north side of Whitley Road, (formerly Front Street, and now Park
View), opposite St Paul's church. The original building was described as 'thatched and picturesque'
and was one of the earliest known pubs in Whitley Bay.
  The first inn was rebuilt in 1869 and again in 1928, the present structure of which is indicated by the
presence of a carved stone plaque above the corner door, which combines the initials 'J.B.' with the

An early view of the Esplanade Hotel in 1905.

date. The initials are those of John Buchanan, the owner/proprietor at the time. The pub underwent a refit in 1985, and in 1995 it was renamed as 'The Tap & Spile' by the new owners; however, after considerable local opposition to the name change, the owners were pressurised to revert back to the original name of the Fat Ox within a very short time.

FIRE STATION (WETHERSPOONS), YORK ROAD, WHITLEY BAY
First recorded in 2000; last recorded in 2007.
After conversion and structural work in 2000, one of the newest public houses in Whitley Bay was so named because the premises formerly housed the old Whitley fire station. Although the main entrance is on Whitley Road, the premises extend to the rear onto York Road.

FITZGERALDS, OXFORD STREET AND 2 SOUTH PARADE, WHITLEY BAY
First recorded in 1992; last recorded in 2007.
Situated on the corner of South Parade and Oxford Street, the premises, occupied by Fitzgeralds, was built as the Exchange Buildings in 1910 and for many years was occupied by William Laws, who ran a large hardware business consisting of a shop to the lower floor with a café upstairs.
During the 1960s, the café became a nightclub which was popularly known as 'the Compass Club'. Over the years, other shops have occupied the site, and following a fire in 1972, the building lay empty until the early 1990s, when it was taken over by the pub chain of Sir John Fitzgerald and converted into a public house.

HIGH POINT HOTEL, PROMENADE, WHITLEY BAY
First recorded in 1912; last recorded in 2005.
Originally built as the Cliffe Hotel prior to 1912 and later renamed the High Point Hotel, this building is situated on the Promenade between Whitley and Cullercoats and occupies a prominent position overlooking the sea, above Table Rocks. The premises closed in 2005 and are to be sold for redevelopment.

The old Broadway Road in around 1900, showing the first Quarry Inn, with Marden House visible to the extreme left.

KITTIWAKE, 11 CLAREMONT CRESCENT, WHITLEY BAY
First recorded in 1961; last recorded in 2007.
A modern styled public house situated within the local shopping centre, the Kittiwake was built in 1961 specifically to cater for the residents of the then newly constructed Whitley Lodge Estate.

LAST ORDERS (REFER TO: RAILWAY INN), HILLHEADS ROAD AND KINGSLEY AVENUE, WHITLEY HILL HEADS

QUARRY INN, BROADWAY, WHITLEY BAY
First recorded in 1854-1927 (Old Quarry Inn).
Prior to the 1920s, the route of the original Broadway between Tynemouth and Whitley ran past the entrance to Marden House and Quarry. This section of road is still in evidence today. The first Quarry Inn was situated on the west side of this road, directly next to the entrance to Marden Quarry. In 1922, the Broadway was realigned and straightened, thus bypassing the old inn, which was demolished a few years later.

QUARRY INN, MARDEN ROAD SOUTH, WHITLEY BAY
Last recorded in 1927-2007 (New Quarry Inn).
In 1927, after the realignment of the new Broadway Road, the second Quarry Inn was commissioned, and construction work started during this year. The inn was built on Marden Road South, at the corner with Burnside Road, and almost directly opposite where the former inn of the same name stood.

RAILWAY INN (REFER TO: CROWN & THISTLE), HILLHEADS ROAD, WHITLEY HILL HEADS

RAILWAY INN, HILLHEADS ROAD AND KINGSLEY AVENUE, WHITLEY HILL HEADS
First recorded in 1927–2006 as The Railway; last recorded in 2006–2007 as Last Orders.
In 1927, the new Railway Inn was constructed on its present site, to replace the original Railway Inn (formerly the Crown & Thistle), which stood further to the west. The inn retained its name from the goods sidings at Monkseaton railway station, which at one time stood towards the rear of the building. In 2006 the pub underwent a full refurbishment which included a name change to the unflattering name of 'Last Orders'.

Hidden away in Algernon Place, the Rockcliff Arms is still one of Whitley Bay's best-kept secrets. This picture dates to around 1910.

REX HOTEL (REFER TO: WAVERLEY HOTEL), ESPLANADE AND PROMENADE, WHITLEY BAY

ROCKCLIFF ARMS, ALGERNON PLACE, WHITLEY BAY
First recorded in 1896; last recorded in 2007.
Situated on the south-east side of Algernon Place, Whitley Bay, the Rockcliff Arms takes its name from the nearby area on the seafront which is generally known and referred to as Rockcliff, where there is a slight corruption of the spelling from 'Rockcliffe'. Although the basic structure remains unaltered, the building has been modified over the years. In addition to the corner doors, there was at one time a set of entrance doors situated in the centre of the pub frontage which led to a very shallow and narrow bar area. The photograph shows these doors, and also indicates that the upstairs floor was at one time billiard rooms.

In recent years the pub has been completely refurbished and renovated and the old bar, buffet and snug rooms converted to an open-plan aspect. This pub is one of the few establishments still existing in the area which retains the charm and character of a traditional inn.

ROYAL HOTEL, EAST PARADE, WHITLEY BAY
First recorded in around 1900; last recorded in 2007.
Originally a residential hotel dating to the early 1900s, this building has undergone a number of changes and alterations over the years, and now incorporates a modern theme bar which is open to non-residents.

SHIP, FRONT STREET, WHITLEY
First recorded in 1811; last recorded in 2007.
There have been three Ship Inns at Whitley, the original being a single-storey whitewashed stone building situated on the corner of Front Street (Whitley Road) and Park Road. The inn was completely rebuilt in 1899, and was only twenty-five years old when it was demolished again in order to rebuild the present curved corner structure on the same site. During the mid-1990s, the traditional character of The Ship was lost when it was turned into a theme pub with an Australian accent along with a name change to 'Bar Oz'. This change was presumably intended to attract the growing trend of young lager drinkers: however, its success appears to have been limited, as this name ran for only a few years.

The second Ship, Whitley Bay, in 1919.

Further efforts to revive its popularity prompted a further name change to 'Dundees', but this was also short-lived and as the pub struggled on, it was once again renamed, this time as 'The Town House'. So many futile name changes are meaningless to the local folk who always remember and call it by the name it carried for almost 200 years – 'The Ship'.

SOUTH PARADE, WHITLEY BAY

South Parade was originally a residential street of large houses with walled gardens and ornamental wrought-iron fences, which were occupied by some of the more affluent people of the town. No public houses ever existed there. The numerous 'pubs' and 'bars' which now line the street are simply a modern development originating from the 1940s and '50s, when many of the large residences were adapted to become bed and breakfast accommodation, catering for the holiday trade of the period.

In the years that followed, the owners extended the houses by taking over adjacent properties, and converting them into larger 'hotels'. Those that were subsequently granted liquor licences were often able to open the bars to non-residents, and so the potential for sales of drink grew. By the 1980s, much of South Parade had therefore evolved into theme bars and 'fun pubs', where many of the owners and names tend to change on a frequent basis. As such, none of these premises have been included here because, strictly speaking, they do not fall into the category of a true pub.

SQUARE AND COMPASS, BATES ISLAND, WHITLEY BAY
First recorded in 1861; last recorded in 1895.

The only public house that ever existed on Bates (St Mary's) Island was The Square and Compass, which was run by a George Ewan and his family. George Ewan was a fisherman who originated from Aberdeen and in 1855 he was granted permission to build a cottage on the island which he later converted into an inn to supplement his income. It was around 1861 that the inn first came into existence, which he called 'the Square and Compass'. The symbolism in the name suggests a Masonic connection, although it is not known if George Ewan was a Freemason, or why the inn was so named. During the 1890s the inn became a popular venue, and many customers caused disruption as they trespassed on neighbouring farm land in order to access the inn. Objections were subsequently made, as a result of which the landowner, Lord Hastings, evicted the Ewan Family in 1895 and the inn subsequently closed.

Above: The Station Hotel, Whitley Road, 1912. The crowd in the foreground have gathered to join in the Patrol Boat Procession.

Below: 'The Vic' in 1890.

STATION HOTEL, WHITLEY ROAD AND ESPLANADE, WHITLEY BAY
First recorded in 1904; last recorded in 2007.
Built in 1904, and situated on the corner of Whitley Road and The Esplanade, the Station Hotel was one of the larger licensed hotels in Whitley Bay. A popular hostelry during the holiday season, it was named because of its close proximity to Whitley Bay railway station.

VICTORIA HOTEL (REFER TO: WHITLEY PARK INN), FRONT STREET (WHITLEY ROAD), WHITLEY BAY

WAVERLEY HOTEL, ESPLANADE AND PROMENADE, WHITLEY BAY
First recorded in 1907; last recorded in 2007.
Originally a temperance hotel, construction work on the Waverley began in 1907. With a huge frontage, the building dominated a site on the Promenade extending around the corner into South Parade, and, over a short time span, incorporated neighbouring houses to become the size it is today. By the late 1920s, it was advertised as one of the largest and most modern residential hotels in the area, having 150 bedrooms. During the 1930s, a liquor licence was granted which allowed the sale and consumption of alcohol for the first time in the hotel's history. This was soon followed by a name change to the better-known Rex Hotel.

WHITLEY PARK HOTEL, WHITLEY BAY
First recorded in 1834; last recorded in 1922.
Whitley Park Hotel stood in Whitley Park, the area of land to the rear of the present library and opposite the former Avenue Hotel. Originally built as a mansion house, an advertisement dated 1842 indicates that the house was to be sold by private contract, and described the property as a desirable mansion house together with a park or close of old grassland immediately behind, containing, with the plantation to the west, six and a half acres of land, a greenhouse and flower garden to the west of the house and a large garden to the east enclosed with a high wall, well-stocked with fruit trees, containing vinery, peach houses etc; also a gardener's cottage and every other convenience. The out-offices consist of servants' apartments, a brewhouse and dairy, stabling for six horses, a roomy coach house and harness room and every other requisite, including an abundant supply of the most delightful spring water, on the whole comprising an area of eleven acres.

The house was purchased and opened as a hotel in 1896 under the supervision of a Miss Carrie Sokell. During the First World War it was requisitioned as a billet for soldiers, and by the end of the war it had been left in a poor state of repair: it was never refurbished, and was eventually purchased by Whitley Council in 1922 before being demolished soon afterwards to lay out the present Whitley Park.

WHITLEY PARK INN, FRONT STREET, WHITLEY VILLAGE
First recorded in 1832-1887 as Whitley Park Inn; 1887-2005 as The Victoria; last recorded in 2007 as The Bedroom.
Standing prominently on the main street through Whitley Bay, the Whitley Park Inn was at one time the largest and most popular inn in Whitley, and is one of the oldest in the town. It was extended in around 1870 to incorporate adjoining cottages and renamed 'The Victoria', which for many years was locally known as 'The Vic'. In 1888, further alterations saw the addition of a third storey to the building, and in 1930, a new Tudor-style frontage was added, followed by the later construction of four stone bay windows. Sadly, what was once a fine building fell victim to the theme bar craze of the twenty-first century, during which the pub has taken what many people would consider a downturn with brightly coloured out-of-character paintwork and signage, and has been tastelessly renamed 'The Bedroom'.

Chapter Eight

Monkseaton

BEACON HOTEL, EARSDON ROAD, WEST MONKSEATON
First recorded in 1957; last recorded in 2007.
Situated on the west side of Earsdon Road, West Monkseaton, the Beacon Hotel was built in 1957, and was so named due to the fact that when it was built, the beacon of St Mary's Lighthouse was clearly visible across the then open fields.

BLACK HORSE, 8 CORONATION ROW AND FRONT STREET, MONKSEATON
First recorded in 1793; last recorded in 2007.
Dating to 1793, and originally built as a two-storey building, the Black Horse Inn was later remodelled to include a third floor. The building stood on the north side of Front Street, Monkseaton, and was demolished in 1936 but immediately rebuilt on the same site. It still stands to this day.

GRANGE HOTEL, EARSDON ROAD, WEST MONKSEATON
First recorded in 1936-1962 as The Grange Hotel; last recorded in 1962-2007 as The Hunting Lodge.
Situated on the west side of Earsdon Road, West Monkseaton, and built in 1936 along with much of the housing in the same area of West Monkseaton, The Grange Hotel was named as such because it stood on land forming part of Monkseaton Grange Farm. Outwardly, the building retains the same appearance as when it was first built as there have been no external additions; however, after undergoing some interior renovations and improvements, The Grange was given the meaningless name of 'The Hunting Lodge' in 1962.

HUNTING LODGE (REFER TO: GRANGE HOTEL), EARSDON ROAD, WEST MONKSEATON

MONKSEATON ARMS, FRONT STREET, MONKSEATON
First recorded in 1683; last recorded in 2007.
Monkseaton Brewery stood on the north side of Front Street, and was built in 1683 for a Michael Turpin of Murton. At that time it was the largest and most conspicuous building in Monkseaton, with whitewashed walls, a red pantiled roof and a tall chimney, which could be seen for many miles around. During this time, Michael Turpin bought a cottage, which adjoined the brewery buildings. This cottage was later to become the first 'Monkseaton Arms'. During 1855, the brewery came into the possession of a William Davison, who resided next door at Monkseaton House. Two reservoirs were built in the rear garden of this house in order to supply the brewery with water. In 1900, the premises were taken over by the Northumberland Brewery Co., who in 1934 sold them to the Newcastle Breweries. Shortly afterwards, the brewery buildings and public house were demolished to make way for the present Monkseaton Arms.

The artist and date of this painting showing The Black Horse Inn, Monkseaton are unknown: however, this scene would be typical of how the village looked around the early to mid-1800s.

RED HOUSE FARM (REFER TO: SHIELING), HEPSCOTT DRIVE, WEST MONKSEATON

SEVEN STARS, THE FOLD, MONKSEATON
First recorded in: unknown; last recorded in 1814.
The Seven Stars was an old inn which stood on the south-east corner of The Fold, Monkseaton, on what is now the corner of Front Street and Rosebery Terrace, close to the present Ship Inn. Little is known of this pub, other than references to a sale notice of 1814 which advertise that it was to be let, and a schedule of the premises indicating there was a cock-fighting pit with glass lights behind. The inn was demolished soon after 1814, and single-storey cottages forming part of The Fold were built in its place. The site is now occupied by sheltered housing called Rosebery Court.

SHIELING, HEPSCOTT DRIVE, WEST MONKSEATON
First recorded in 1987-2003 as The Shieling; last recorded in 2003-2007 as The Red House Farm.
A shieling is a hut or shelter for shepherds or fishermen. Built in a shape similar to an octagon, The Shieling public house was built in 1987 along with the housing project which saw much of the development of Red House Farm Estate. In 2003, the building was updated and took a change of name to The Red House Farm.

SHIP INN, PERCY TERRACE, MONKSEATON
First recorded in 1790; last recorded in 2007.
Originally a farmhouse built in 1688 as part of Monkseaton Dairy Farm, and standing on the site of what is now the junction of Percy Terrace and Lyndhurst Road, the first Ship Inn came into being in 1790 when it was converted to a public house. In 1922, the building was demolished and construction work started on the present Ship Inn, which was built for the Northumberland Brewery Co., (the then owners of Monkseaton Brewery) on a site slightly to the west, at the edge of Rosebery Terrace. Building work was completed a year later, and a plaque above the door reads: '1688, Ye Olde Ship Inn. Rebuilt 1923'. In 1934, Newcastle Breweries acquired the building from the Northumberland Brewery Co. Externally, the building has changed very little, but there have been several interior alterations over the years.

The Black Horse, after rebuilding in 1936.

Monkseaton Arms: The first Monkseaton Arms adjoined the Northumberland Brewery, and stood on the site of what is now part of the present pub car park. This picture dates to around 1912.

The original Ship Inn, *c.* 1910.

Three Horse Shoes Inn, *c.* 1900.

THREE HORSE SHOES INN, CHAPEL LANE, MONKSEATON
First recorded in 1795; last recorded in 1857.

The Three Horse Shoes Inn stood on the west side of Chapel Lane, not far from the junction with Front Street. The building dates from 1795 when it opened as an alehouse under the name of 'The Three Horse Shoes'. During its lifetime, it has been an inn, a shop, a post office and a private residence. It was rebuilt in the early 1930s as a private detached residence, which was latterly referred to as 'Garnick's Cottage', named as such after the last resident. This house had fell into disrepair and was demolished in 1998 to be replaced by a new detached house which stands on the corner of Chapel Lane at its junction with the back lane of Front Street.

Chapter Nine

Cullercoats

BAY HOTEL (REFER TO: HUDDLESTON ARMS HOTEL), HUDDLESTON STREET/
FRONT STREET, CULLERCOATS

BORDER TERRIER, HARTINGTON ROAD, TYNEMOUTH
First recorded in 1960; last recorded in 2007.
A relatively modern pub built by Thomas Clements & Sons for Scottish Brewers Ltd in 1960, the
Border Terrier was constructed to complement the nearby Magpie and accommodate the needs of
the residents of Marden Estate. The building stands on the north side of Hartington Road at the
junction with Honister Road.

DOVE INN, CULLERCOATS
First recorded in: unknown; last recorded in 1792.
In 1893, William Weaver Tomlinson wrote a book entitled *Historical Notes on Cullercoats, Whitley and
Monkseaton*, which refers to the existence of an inn 'known by the sign of the Dove' in 1792. It has
not been established exactly where the inn was situated, although there is little doubt that it would
have had a connection with the prominent Dove family, who were instrumental in the development
of Cullercoats in the seventeenth century.

HOPE AND ANCHOR, CULLERCOATS
First recorded in 1822; last recorded in 1828.
There are very few historical references to this inn, which was known to exist in Cullercoats in the
early 1800s, and no indications of exactly where it was situated.

HUDDLESTON ARMS HOTEL, HUDDLESTON STREET AND FRONT STREET,
CULLERCOATS
*First recorded in 1870-1893 as The Huddleston Arms; last recorded in 1893-2005 as the Bay
Hotel.*
The Huddleston Arms Hotel stood on the site of an older building called The Ship Inn, which
was demolished in 1868. The new hotel opened in 1870, the name of which originated from the
prominent local Huddleston family. In 1893, several alterations were carried out, and the hotel was
renamed The Cullercoats Bay Hotel, but by the 1930s, 'Cullercoats' had been dropped from the name
and it had become better known as simply The Bay Hotel.

It was an impressive building, situated on the bank top overlooking the sea across Cullercoats Bay.
A number of other alterations over the years saw a change in the external appearance, with the loss of
balconies and frontages. The building was demolished in 2005, and replaced by modern apartments.

MAGPIE, HARTINGTON ROAD, TYNEMOUTH
First recorded in 1960; last recorded in 2007.
Built in 1960 at the same time as the nearby Border Terrier, the Magpie is situated on the corner of Hartington Road and Kirklinton Road. It was named as a tribute to Newcastle United Football Club.

NEWCASTLE ARMS, 48 FRONT STREET, CULLERCOATS
First recorded in 1844; last recorded in 1973.
The Newcastle Arms was situated on the west side of Front Street, Cullercoats, next to and to the north of The Bay Hotel. The first directory reference is dated 1844 and mentions the 'Castle Arms'; however this is probably a misspelling of the name. After almost 130 years in existence, the pub was demolished in 1973, and the site was developed as a car park for the neighbouring Bay Hotel.

PIPER, FARRINGDON ROAD, CULLERCOATS
First recorded in 1964; last recorded in 2007.
Built on land which was once part of Marden Farm, the Piper is situated on the north-east corner of Farringdon Road at its junction with Shaftesbury Crescent. It was a purpose-built pub intended to serve the residents of Marden Farm Estate and was opened on 10 March 1964 by Captain R.J. Bowler, of the Black Watch.

QUEENS HEAD, 6 FRONT STREET, CULLERCOATS
First recorded in 1813; last recorded in 2007.
The Queens Head is situated on the east side of Front Street, close to the bank top at Cullercoats. The building has undergone a number of alterations during its lifetime, and some of the original stone walls are still incorporated within the present structure.

SHIP INN (SHIP HOTEL), 38 FRONT STREET, CULLERCOATS
First recorded in 1746; last recorded in the 1970s.
There were two Ship Inns in Cullercoats, one of which occupied the site on which The Huddleston Arms or Bay Hotel formerly stood. Despite the confusion which must have been caused with two pubs of the same name in the village, this particular three-storey inn, stood on the west side of Front Street, near to Browns Buildings. It was demolished during the 1970s.

SHIP INN, CULLERCOATS
First recorded in the 1700s; last recorded in 1868.
There was a Ship Inn recorded in Cullercoats which occupied part of the site on which the Huddlestone Arms (Bay Hotel) formerly stood. Little is known of this building, which was demolished in 1868.

Opposite above: Huddleston Arms Hotel, later known as The Bay Hotel, *c.* 1920.

Opposite below: Front Street, Cullercoats, *c.* 1906. The large building on the left is the Newcastle Arms.

Chapter Ten

Earsdon, Shiremoor and Backworth

BACKWORTH HOTEL, BACKWORTH LANE, BACKWORTH
First recorded in 1860; last recorded in 2003.
Situated on the south side of Backworth Lane, the Backworth Hotel was built around 1860 by the Duke of Northumberland. In recent years the name was changed to Deuchars, after the Scottish brewing company, but trade declined and the premises closed in 2003.

BEAUMONT, PARK LANE, SHIREMOOR
First recorded in the 1950s; last recorded in 2007.

BEEHIVE INN, HARTLEY LANE, EARSDON
First recorded in 1896; last recorded in 2007.
In 1730, two adjoining cottages were built on Hartley Lane, Earsdon to house the clerks who managed Lord Delavals' estates, and as a result, they were colourfully referred to as 'Clarks' Houses'. These houses were vacated in 1815 and taken over by a Quaker family, who made several alterations and modified the buildings to establish a dairy farm. In 1896, the farm was converted into a public house, which was named 'The Beehive', the first licensee of which was a James Linfoot. Most of the ales supplied to the pub in its early years were supplied by the Monkseaton Brewery. A tall pole stood to the rear of the pub, and during the First and Second World Wars, a flag was raised to full mast indicating to the residents of the nearby villages of Wellfield, Earsdon, Holywell and Old Hartley that an ample supply of ales was available! In 1986, The Beehive became a listed building, which still manages to retain the charm and character of an 'olde world' hostelry with low doors and ceiling beams.

BLUE BELL, EARSDON ROAD, SHIREMOOR
First recorded in 1891; last recorded in 2007.
The Blue Bell stands on the south side of Earsdon Road, Shiremoor, and was named after the nearby Blue Bell Pit. For many years until the 1970s, the well-known Blue Bell railway crossing also stood directly next to the pub. A notice dated 25 August 1891 advertises the Blue Bell Shiremoor, situated at Nos 6, 7 and 8 Hotspur Place (Earsdon Road), for sale by auction, with the premises comprising a bar, four rooms with a large larder to the ground floor, a cellar to the basement, a large club room and three other rooms to the first floor with a yard, out-offices and a garden.

CANNON INN, FRONT STREET, EARSDON
First recorded in 1815; last recorded in 2007.
Tucked away in a corner, the Cannon Inn is situated on the south side of the road towards the western extremity of Front Street, Earsdon. It is believed that an inn has existed on this site since at least 1753 and although no written documentation seems to exist, it may at one time have been called

The first Dun Cow Inn, New York Village, *c.* 1890.

The Grey Horse, Bartram Place, Shiremoor in 1983.

Front Street, Earsdon, looking west in 1904. The large white building to the centre of the picture is the Phoenix Inn.

The Spread Eagle Inn. An auction sale notice dated 1881 advertises the premises as a dwelling house and garden, which was subsequently sold for the sum of £840. By 1900, it had been purchased by Camerons' Brewery with a small portion of adjoining land. In 1975, The Cannon Inn underwent extensive interior renovation and alteration work, which is reflected inside the pub today.

DEUCHARS (REFER TO: BACKWORTH HOTEL), BACKWORTH LANE, BACKWORTH

DUN COW, NEW YORK ROAD, NEW YORK
First recorded in 1828 (at Preston – refer to 'Dun Cow', Preston); last recorded in 1903-2007 (present building).
The original Dun Cow was situated on New York Road, and was rebuilt on its present site in 1903 for a William Currell. Some old notes dated 1828 show a Red Cow listed in Murton: however, it is likely that the name of this inn should actually read 'The Dun Cow'. The word *Dun* is rarely used these days, and is derived from Middle English, meaning an almost neutral brownish-grey to dull greyish-brown colour.

GREY HORSE, BARTRAM PLACE, SHIREMOOR
First recorded in 1841; last recorded in 2007.
The Grey Horse is situated on Bartram Place, Shiremoor at the junction with Earsdon Lane (now Earsdon Road).

NORTHUMBERLAND ARMS, THE ALLOTMENT
First recorded in 1828; last recorded in 2007.
Situated on the south side of Benton Road, west allotment, the Northumberland Arms was first recorded in 1828 and still operates as a public house.

PHOENIX, FRONT STREET, EARSDON
First recorded in 1822; last recorded in 1971.
A mythical bird that dies in flames and is reborn from the ashes lends its name to this pub, which stood on the north side of Earsdon Front Street, virtually opposite the old coach house and next to Taylor's Cottages. Built during the eighteenth century, the Phoenix was a double-fronted, two-storey inn built from lime-washed rubble walling with a pantiled roof and faced directly onto the road.

As the building was constructed on a slight incline, there was a variation of twelve inches in the floor levels, as a result of which two passageway steps rose from front to back. The cellar was hewn out of solid rock, the bar was situated to the left of the main front entrance door, and a public room was situated to the right of the entrance. The inn closed its doors for the last time at 10.30 p.m. on 7 December 1971. It was advertised for sale and purchased by a property developer who converted the building into two private dwelling houses, with the old rubble frontage being refaced in stone leaf.

PLOUGH INN, FRONT STREET, EARSDON
First recorded in 1822; last recorded in 1834.
The Plough Inn was situated behind the north side of Front Street, almost opposite the present Cannon Inn, and within the area of Earsdon Town Farm. In 1822, the occupant was a John Buchan, who, in addition to being a farmer, converted part of the farmhouse, which he named the Plough Inn. The pub lasted for at least twelve years, as the last recorded date for its existence was 1834, after which, the buildings of Town Farm were demolished and rebuilt (*c.* 1872).

PLOUGH, MURTON VILLAGE
First recorded in 1828; last recorded in 1828.
This inn is recorded in some notes dated 1828, but nothing is known of it or its exact location.

Looking north on Holywell Lane, Earsdon, the original Red Lion Inn can be seen to the centre of the picture with a cart standing outside.

RED LION, HOLYWELL LANE
First recorded in 1822; last recorded in 1939.

The Red Lion is widely regarded as the most common name for an English pub. Pubs are often named after heraldic animals and devices, of which the lion is particularly common. Several lions appear in the arms of the United Kingdom, but, ironically enough, the only red one appears in the arms of Scotland.

The first Red Lion at Earsdon was located on the west side of the Earsdon to Holywell road, about 100 yards from the present junction with Front Street. A stone building with the manager's quarters upstairs, it closed as a public house in 1939 and was converted into a shop, and later to a dwelling house. It was replaced by the present Red Lion Inn during the same year.

RED LION, FRONT STREET, EARSDON
First recorded in 1939; last recorded in 2007.

The present Red Lion was built in 1939 and replaced the old inn of the same name, which stood about 100 yards away on the west side of the Earsdon to Holywell road.

ROBIN HOOD, WELL LANE, MURTON VILLAGE
First recorded in 1849; last recorded in 2007.

Named after the legendary folk hero who is reputed to have lived in Sherwood Forest, the Robin Hood is situated in the centre of the village. The property was advertised for sale in February 1849 as 'a pub known by the sign of the Robin Hood, containing four rooms, a back kitchen and cellar with a stable attached'.

This photograph of the Robin Hood Inn, Murton, was taken around the turn of the century. The group of men standing at the door were all residents of the village.

TRAVELLERS' REST, NEW YORK ROAD AND MURTON LANE, NEW YORK
First recorded in 1855; last recorded in 1858.
A directory of 1855 and an Ordnance Survey map of 1858 shows an inn by the name of the Travellers' Rest, located on the north side of New York Road next to the old smithy at the junction with Murton Lane. No other records appear to exist in relation to this pub.

WHEATSHEAF, BACKWORTH LANE, BACKWORTH
First recorded in 1834; last recorded in 1834.
There is an absence of records relating to this pub, which according to early Ordnance Survey maps was situated on Backworth Lane, behind the Backworth Hotel (later Deuchars).

WHEATSHEAF, NEW YORK ROAD
First recorded in 1827; last recorded in 2007.
There is a suggestion that an inn has stood on this site since 1787; however, the first record is of the Wheatsheaf in 1827, when an auction notice dated 23 August advertises the sale of: 'A field of excellent wheat containing 20 acres adjoining the above premises'. The inn is situated on the north side of New York Road at its junction with Murton Lane, which at one time was a section of the old main road running through New York Village and connecting the coast with West Allotment, Shiremoor and Backworth.

Chapter Eleven

Beer Merchants and Retailers

Some inns and taverns would have an off-sales area attached to the premises, which was sometimes known as a 'bottle and jug', or family room, where ales, spirits and drinks could be purchased and taken away to be consumed off the premises. There were also a large number of ale, porter, wine and spirit merchants in the district, who operated independently of the public houses, from shops and premises which today would perhaps amount to the equivalent of an off-licence. The list of merchants and retailers shown below has been compiled from information recorded in old trade directories: however, it is by no means a comprehensive listing.

Under the appropriate heading, details are shown in alphabetical order of surname, followed by the premises' address and the years of trading.

ALE AND PORTER MERCHANTS

Hall & Co. Ltd	Albion Road, North Shields.	1899-1911
Holliday, J.S. & Co.	26 Prudhoe Street, North Shields.	1887-1899
Riggall, S.	29 Camden Street, North Shields.	1887
Russell, R.	24 Stanley Street, North Shields.	1899
Russell, Robt.	20 Borough Road, North Shields.	1887

ALE AND PORTER MERCHANTS, WINE AND SPIRIT MERCHANTS AND IMPORTERS

Duffy, P.	Nile Street, North Shields.	1855
Lamb, J. & Co.	18 William Street, North Shields.	1899
Rees, J. & Co.	21 Bedford Street, North Shields.	1887-1940
Wilkinson, Wm. Arth.	50 King Street & George Street, North Shields.	1887-1930

BEERHOUSE KEEPERS

Avery, A.	4 Stephenson Street, North Shields.	1887
Battensby, Thos.	57 Camden Street, North Shields.	1887
Bell, W.	1 Grey Street, North Shields.	1887
Brown, Eliz.	41 Tyne Street, North Shields.	1887
Brown, James	Northumberland Street, North Shields.	1855
Brown, Wm.	Ropery Banks, North Shields.	1887
Campbell, Joseph	54 Bedford Street, North Shields.	1887
Carnaby, W.	Nelson Street, North Shields.	1855
Coffton, B.	Camden Street, North Shields.	1855
Cook, W.	Duke Street, North Shields.	1855
Dawson, Jno.	83 Hudson Street, North Shields.	1887
Dennison, Hannah	Charlotte Street, North Shields.	1855

Doubleday, J.	Linskill Street, North Shields.	1855
Flinn, Ed.	24 West Percy Street, North Shields.	1855
Gray, Mrs C.	56 Grey Street, North Shields.	1887
Hogg, E.	Percy Street, North Shields.	1855
Mansfield, Geo.	Collingwood Street, North Shields.	1887
McDowell, M.	12 Wellington Street, North Shields.	1887
Openshaw Bros.	Albion Road, North Shields.	1887
Petrie, John	Bell Street, North Shields.	1855
Sands, G.	1 Saville Street West, North Shields.	1887
Scott, G.	Church Way, North Shields.	1855
Scott, T.	Upper Pearson Street, North Shields.	1855
Stewardson, Wm.	86 Clive Street, North Shields.	1887
Stewart, G.H.	7 Saville Street, North Shields.	1855
Stonebank, Reed	Stephenson Street, North Shields.	1855
Strong, A.	South Street, North Shields.	1855
Strong, Jas.	68 George Street, North Shields.	1887
Thompson, W.	Albion Road, North Shields.	1887
Varley, H.	Cullercoats.	1855
Whitfield, J.	Saville Street, North Shields.	1855
Wood, John	Clive Street, North Shields.	1855

BEER RETAILERS

Ainsley, John	32 Hudson Street, North Shields.	1834
Armstrong, J.	4 Spencer Street, North Shields.	1928
Armstrong, Mary M.	44 Norfolk Street, North Shields.	1887
Auty, M.	1 William Street and 94 Prudhoe Street, N. Shields.	1928–1940
Baker, Geo.	2 Albert Terrace, North Shields.	1887
Baxter, H.	1 Saville Street West, North Shields.	1928–1936
Bell, A.	2 Albert Terrace, North Shields.	1912
Berryman, C.	63 Stephenson Street, North Shields.	1887
Boys, T.	12 Newcastle Street, North Shields.	1912
Brownlee, J.	21 Victoria Street, North Shields.	1912
Burrough, Mrs A.M.	4 Spencer Street, North Shields.	1940
Calder, J.T.	4 Nile Street, North Shields.	1928–1930
Carey, A.D.	18 Penman Street, North Shields.	1928–1936
Clements, Mrs M.A.	5 Wellington Street West, North Shields.	1912
Cochrane, Mrs E.	4 Spencer Street, North Shields.	1936
Common, John	Brunswick Place, North Shields.	1834
Cowey, Mrs M.	57 Camden Street, North Shields.	1928
Cowey, R.H.	57 Camden Street, North Shields.	1912
Cragg, A.W.	15 Prudhoe Street, North Shields.	1928–1936
Crammond, R.	30 Bell Street, North Shields.	1887
Crowthers, Robt S.	6 Nile Street, North Shields.	1887–1940
Davie, G.B.	10 Spencer Street, North Shields.	1887
Dixon, Mrs M.A.	41 Tyne Street, North Shields.	1928
Dixon, W.A.	85 Howdon Road, North Shields.	1912
Dunleavy, Mrs R.	2 Stephenson Street, North Shields.	1912
Dunn, T.	Tennyson Terrace, North Shields.	1928–1940

Durham and Northumberland

Licensed Victuallers' Synd.	6 Saville Street West, North Shields.	1936-1940
English, J.	13 Coburg Street, North Shields.	1912-1928
Euen, Wm.	43 Church Street, North Shields.	1887
Farrow, Mrs C.	50 Rudyerd Street, North Shields.	1928
Forster, R.	33 West Percy Street, North Shields.	1912
Fraser, C.	12 Wellington Street, North Shields.	1928
Gamble, J.	6 Saville Street West, North Shields.	1928-1930
Gilbertson, T.S.	41 Tyne Street, North Shields.	1930-1936
Gladders, W.	Tynemouth Road, North Shields.	1930
Gladders, W.	50 Nile Street, North Shields.	1936-1940
Graham, Mrs D.	44 Norfolk Street, North Shields.	1930
Gray, Mary	North Street, North Shields.	1834
Grounsell, C.E.	85 Howdon Road, North Shields.	1928-1930
Hall, H.B.	94 Prudhoe Street, North Shields.	1928
Hay, E.	1 Grey Street, North Shields.	1912
Heppell, Mrs E.	6 Nile Street, North Shields.	1912
Hields, Mrs A.	91 Norfolk Street, North Shields.	1928-1940
Hill, Mrs F.A.	50 Rudyerd Street, North Shields.	1930
Hindmarch, W.	44 Sidney Street, North Shields.	1912
Hobkinson, L.	4 Spencer Street, North Shields.	1912
Hough, R.	4 Nile Street, North Shields.	1912
Hudson, W.	4 Spencer Street, North Shields.	1930
Humble, R.	44 Norfolk Street, North Shields.	1912
Hutchinson, Mrs A.	1 Albert Terrace, North Shields.	1912
Hutchinson, Mrs A.	54 Bedford Street, North Shields.	1912
Ingren, A.	14 Middle Street, North Shields.	1912
Jackson, R.H.	Albion Road West, North Shields.	1912
James, J.	14 Middle Street, North Shields.	1887
Johnson, C.G.	2 Albion Road, North Shields.	1912-1936
Lamb, W.	43 Church Street, North Shields.	1912
Lee, Mrs S.	1 Grey Street, North Shields.	1928-1930
Little, W.	1 & 2 Albert Terrace, North Shields.	1928-1940
Long, O.S.	9 Liddell Street, North Shields.	1887
Manson, Thos.	6 Saville Street, North Shields.	1887
Martin, F.L.	13 Coburg Street, North Shields.	1936
McCombie, A.	44 Sidney Street, North Shields.	1928
McCombie, Miss I.	50 Nile Street, North Shields.	1928-1930
McCord, Mrs D.	10 Spencer Street, North Shields.	1936-1940
McGarrity, Mrs M.	Tynemouth Road, North Shields.	1928
McGarrity, Mrs M.	162 Stephenson Street, North Shields.	1912-1930
McHugh, E.	21 Clive Street, North Shields.	1887
Miller, R.	Albion Road West, North Shields.	1928-1930
Morley, Elizabeth	30 Liddell Street, North Shields.	1834
Morris, Mrs C.	162 Stephenson Street, North Shields.	1928
Morrison, J.H.	41 Tyne Street, North Shields.	1912
Mould, C.	4 Stephenson Street, North Shields.	1912
Mould, F.W.	6 Saville Street West, North Shields.	1899-1912
Munro, Miss A.	91 Norfolk Street, North Shields.	1912

Newton, Margaret	Union Street, North Shields.	1834
Newton, Mrs E.	1 Albert Terrace, North Shields.	1928-1930
Patterson, C.R.	13 Coburg Street, North Shields.	1940
Patterson, W.A.	51 Gardner Street, North Shields.	1912
Raine, A.	4 Trinity Street, North Shields.	1928-1930
Ratcliffe, C.H.	68 George Street, North Shields.	1928-1930
Reay, H.W.	15 Bedford Street, North Shields.	1912-1928
Richards, J.T.	Tynemouth Road, North Shields.	1936-1940
Rischmiller, F.	4 Spencer Street, North Shields.	1887
Robinson, J.	45 Lawson Street, North Shields.	1912
Robson, J.R.	2 Albion Road, North Shields.	1940
Ross, R.	68 George Street, North Shields.	1912
Scott, T.	1 Saville Street West, North Shields.	1912
Shipley, Mrs B.	10 Spencer Street, North Shields.	1912
Sleep, F.	47 Dene Street, North Shields.	1928
Smith, E.	9 Newcastle Street, North Shields.	1912
Smith, Mrs E.	50 Rudyerd Street, North Shields.	1936-1940
Snaith, W.D.	47 Dene Street, North Shields.	1930-1936
Stanford, Daniel	48 Clive Street, North Shields.	1834
Stather, L.	162 Stephenson Street, North Shields.	1936
Steel, Annie	162 Stephenson Street, North Shields.	1887
Stephenson, A.	18 Penman Street, North Shields.	1912
Steven, J.R.	50 Rudyerd Street, North Shields.	1912
Strong, Thomas	Brunswick Place, North Shields.	1834
Thompson, Mrs M.	10 Spencer Street, North Shields.	1928-1930
Tinsley, F.	33 West Percy Street, North Shields.	1887
Tuff, Mrs I.	44 Norfolk Street, North Shields.	1928
Turnbull, R.	1 William Street, North Shields.	1887-1912
Turner, Mrs G.	44 Sidney Street, North Shields.	1930
Walker, Jane	94 Prudhoe Street, North Shields.	1887
Watson, Mrs L.	1 Saville Street West, North Shields.	1940
Weatherald, Jas. Sen.	50 Rudyerd Street, North Shields.	1887
Weir, Mrs S.E.	94 Prudhoe Street, North Shields.	1912
White, F.W.	13 Coburg Street, North Shields.	1930
White, J.T.	12 Wellington Street West, North Shields.	1912
Wilson, Thomas	King Street, North Shields.	1834
Woll, A.	18 William Street, North Shields.	1912
Younger, William	Tynemouth.	1834

BREWERS AND MALTSTERS, ALE, PORTER, WINE AND SPIRIT MERCHANTS

Allison, W.H. & Co.	4 Duke Street, North Shields.	1855-1887
Bartleman & Crightons	Bull Ring & Clive Street, North Shields.	1850-1855
Bartleman, Alex	Clive St & (Northumberland Brewery), N. Shields.	1822-1834
Brunton & Falconers	Howdon Panns.	1834
Carr Bros & Carr	Low Lights Brewery & Norfolk Street, N. Shields.	1887
Carr, Ormston & Carr	Low Lights, North Shields.	1855
Cockburn & Nichols	Clive Street, North Shields.	1834
Crawford, John	Low Lights Brewery, North Shields.	1822-1828
Crighton, Alexander & Son Preston		1834

Davison & Son	Monkseaton Brewery, Monkseaton Village.	1855
Dryden, Thos. C.	Bell Street, North Shields & Monkseaton Brewery.	1822–1828
Fenwick, Nicholas	Liddell Street (North Shields Brewery).	1828–1834
Fenwick, Richd	Liddell Street, North Shields.	1822
Harbutt, Thomas	Bull Ring, North Shields.	1834
Harrison, J.	38 Duke Street, North Shields.	1850
Harrison, John	Duke Street, North Shields.	1822–1834
Johnson, William	69 Church Street, North Shields.	1834
Newcastle Breweries Ltd	4 Duke Street, North Shields.	1899–1928
Newton, Margt	Union Street Brewery, North Shields.	1834
Openshaw Bros.	Tynemouth Road, North Shields.	1887–1912
Richardson, James	Duke Street (High Brewery), North Shields.	1828
Richardson, Thomas	Percy Brewery, North Shields.	1834
Robinson, Richard	Low Lights, North Shields.	1834
Roddam, Hugh Robt.	Bell Street, North Shields.	1822–1828
Sinclair, Edward & Co.	Bell Street, North Shields & Monkseaton Brewery.	1834
Stanford, Daniel	Liddell Street, North Shields.	1834
Storey & Cockburn	Bell Street, North Shields.	1834
W. Davison & Son	Monkseaton Brewery, Monkseaton Village.	1850–1855
Walker, Hannah	Bull Ring, North Shields.	1822
Walker, Wm.	Bull Ring (Percy Brewery), North Shields.	1828
Walton, Ralph	Bull Ring, North Shields.	1822–1828

PORTER AND ALE DEALERS

Fairlie, Wm.	Market Place, North Shields.	1822
Marley, Bridget	Dockwray Square, North Shields.	1822
Pringle, Elsdon	Tyne Street, North Shields.	1822
Walton. Thos.	Motley's Quay, Bull Ring, North Shields.	1822

WINE AND SPIRIT MERCHANTS AND IMPORTERS

Atkinson, J.	Clive Street, North Shields.	1855
Blackett, T. Ltd.	21 & 112 West Percy Street, North Shields.	1912–1940
Calverley & Gee	94 Prudhoe Street, North Shields.	1940
Clark, W.N. & Co.	1 Wooden Bridge, North Shields.	1855
Deuchar, R.	69 Church Way, North Shields.	1912
Dodds, A.N.	White Hart, Bedford Street, North Shields.	1887
Donkin, William	19 Clive Street, North Shields.	1834
Dunn, W.	Howard Street, North Shields.	1855
Ewen & Co. Ltd	Cleveland Avenue, North Shields.	1928–1930
Gibson, T.	New Quay, North Shields.	1899
Guildford & Co.	12 & 31 Saville Street, North Shields.	1887–1912
Guildford & Co. Ltd	16 Saville Street, North Shields.	1928–1940
Harbutt, T.	63 Bedford Street, North Shields.	1855
Harbutt, Thomas, Jun.	100 Church Way & Bull Ring, North Shields.	1834
Harrison, John	1 Bird Street, North Shields.	1834
Honeyman, James	Clive Street, North Shields.	1822
Hunter, James	Bell Street, North Shields.	1822
Knott, Matt.	52 Nile Street, North Shields.	1887–1912
Liddell, F.	4 Union Street, North Shields.	1855

Lindsay, Jas.	Corner of Norfolk St & Tyne Street, North Shields.	1834
Mather, John, & Co.	Liddell Street, North Shields.	1834
Mathwin, F.F.	63 Bell Street, North Shields.	1834-1855
Newcastle Breweries Ltd	71 Bedford Street, North Shields.	1930-1940
Peart, Joseph	20 Tyne Street, North Shields.	1822-1834
Potts, R.	69 Church Way, North Shields.	1887
Purvis	1 Camden Street, North Shields.	1855
Reid, J.	3 Clive Street, North Shields.	1887
Richardson, James	Bedford Street, North Shields.	1822
Richardson, James	31 Clive Street, North Shields.	1834
Roddam, Hugh Robert	2 Howard Street, North Shields.	1834
Sharp, John	45 Clive Street, North Shields.	1822-1834
Spiden, John	Bull Ring, North Shields.	1834
Thirlwell, Thomas	4 Bedford Street, North Shields.	1834
Walton, Thos	Morley's Quay, Bull Ring, North Shields.	1822
Weatherley, John	5 Union Street, North Shields.	1822-1834
Whittle, J.L.	Saville Street, North Shields.	1855
Wilkinson & Co.	39 Saville Street, North Shields.	1928

EXTERNALLY DECORATED PUBS

During the early 1900s, many public houses were built and faced with glazed terracotta or decorated ceramic tiles, which were usually accompanied with the name of the establishment displayed in ornate signage and lettering. There were a small number of pubs of this type in North Shields, and one in Tynemouth. They typically had façades that were glazed in varying shades of brown, amber, and yellow, all of which added an attractive and prestigious style and appearance to the building.

Although hard-wearing, this method of building was a very time-consuming and expensive process to undertake. An architect would have to produce a detailed plan in order to prepare for the bricks and tiles to be individually manufactured. This in itself was a lengthy operation, as the finished items would also have to be checked to ensure they all fitted together perfectly. They would then in turn have to be numbered before shipment to make certain that they were correctly constructed on site. There were nine known local public houses which had this style of faience, three of which have been demolished. Of the six remaining, four were still trading as public houses in 2007, and are as follows:

1) The Berwick Arms, Trinity Street, North Shields.	(Still Trading)
2) The Borough Arms, Gardner Street, North Shields.	(Demolished)
3) The Crane House, Duke Street, North Shields.	(Change of use/Preserved)
4) The Crown & Sceptre, Stephenson Street, North Shields.	(Demolished)
5) The Cumberland Arms, Front Street, Tynemouth.	(Still Trading)
6) The Fountain Head, Bedford Street, North Shields.	(Demolished)
7) The Garricks Head, Saville Street, North Shields.	(Still Trading)
8) The Railway, Nile Street, North Shields.	(Converted/Change of use)
9) Tynemouth Lodge Hotel, Tynemouth Road, North Shields.	(Still Trading)

And finally, opposite: The Star and Garter Inn, and the entrance to Star and Garter Quay, *c.* 1895. (North Shields).

Other local titles published by Tempus

Cullercoats
RAY MARSHALL

Winslow Homer wrote of his fascination with Cullercoats people, 'there are none like them in my own country'. Featuring more than 200 archive images, this book provides a unique record of harbour life over the last two centuries. Telling of legendary rescues at sea, and fishwives' stoicism, *Cullercoats* will waken memories for many readers, offering a unique glimpse of the past.

978 07524 4285 3

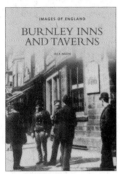

Burnley Inns and Taverns
JACK NADIN

The Industrial Revolution made Burnley the 'Cotton Capital of the World'. Yet the town's new-found fame came at a cost, bringing poverty, strikes and famine that drove many workers to drink. Illustrated with 70 vintage photographs, this book tells the histories of the 300 establishments that they frequented. With tales of violence, robbery and drunkenness, this is an essential guide to the inns and taverns of Burnley.

978 07524 4413 0

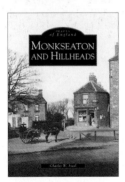

Monkseaton and Hillheads
CHARLIE STEEL

This fascinating collection of 200 archive photographs illustrates some of the history of these two towns over the last century. The images show streets and buildings, schools and churches, people at work and play and feature some famous personalities from the town's past, providing a vital record of life in the area as it used to be.

978 07524 2064 6

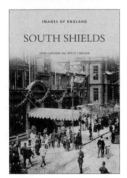

South Shields
JOHN CARLSON AND JOYCE CARLSON

This fascinating selection of more than 190 images captures some of the changes seen in South Shields over the years. Once a hub of the ship-building and coal-mining trades, the town has witnessed the demise of these industries and had to adjust to new businesses, promoting itself as a seaside resort. A vital record of South Shields' past, the book is sure to evoke nostalgic memories for anyone who has worked or lived in the town.

978 07524 4077 4

If you are interested in purchasing other books published by Tempus, or in case you have difficulty finding any Tempus books in your local bookshop, you can also place orders directly through our website

www.tempus-publishing.com